Praise for *What's Next?*

"Bill Leider's *What's Next?* is an illuminating voyage into self-discovery and personal transformation. Leider is the ultimate navigator, guiding readers toward a deeper understanding of themselves by combining cutting-edge neuroscience with valuable experiential insights. His work echoes the wisdom shared by an Indian sage: 'The greatest exploration one will ever make is the realization within.'

What's Next? offers readers an essential map to navigate this inward journey, unlocking the potential for profound growth and change.

On a more personal note, a Divine Hand works in wondrous and unexpected ways, often when we least expect it. Following the loss in our family and in the midst of uncertainty both personally and collectively, *What's Next?* has been a North Star!"

—Elizabeth Lindsey, PhD, cultural anthropologist
and United Nations Visionary Award recipient

"Bill Leider's latest book, *What's Next? How to Make Your Next Chapter Your Best Chapter*, reflects Carl Jung's quote 'Who looks outside dreams. Who looks inside awakens.'

Through stories and the clarity of Leider's writing, *What's Next?* is a guide to awakening what is inside of you: creating your vision, defining your values, understanding your greater purpose—your *why*—and sharing it with others.

Leider's brilliant method for looking inside is to ask the profound question 'What would it take?' The question unleashes creative energy the way $E = mc^2$ unleashes thermonuclear energy. Asking the question, framing it to look inside for the answer, and reflecting on what we find: these form the foundation of our next chapter.

The book is easy to read. It's grounded in neuroscience. It's full of questions for you to ask yourself. It encourages you to be vulnerable—the more vulnerable we allow ourselves to be, the more we awaken. And it offers Leider's own vulnerability as a beautiful role model for us all."

—Stan Stahl, PhD, founder and President,
SecureTheVillage, and author of *The Agnostic Patriot*

"In *What's Next? How to Make Your Next Chapter Your Best Chapter*, Bill Leider combines state-of-the-art neuroscience with intimate insights to create a compelling road map for personal transformation. It is an easy read, seamlessly merging highly personal stories with reflective exercises to demystify complex concepts such as neuroplasticity and emotional regulation. Leider's openness and vulnerability make the material highly relatable, encouraging readers to harness their brain's adaptability to foster real change.

A standout aspect of the book is its practical application of the science behind how our brains work to everyday life. Leider specifically focuses on overcoming the fear of change, a common human trait, by equipping readers with tools to embrace uncertainty through knowledge and curiosity. This makes *What's Next?* an essential read for anyone seeking to understand and improve their emotional and cognitive behaviors. If you're ready to begin a significant and rewarding personal journey, *What's Next?* should be what's next on your reading list."

—Jeff Turner cofounder of Tangilla, and advisor to Venture MLS

"Bill Leider's book *What's Next? How to Make Your Next Chapter Your Best Chapter* is about becoming the best person each of us can be. I read this book shortly after my brother passed away. The book was a great guide to helping me be in the moment and grow in my awareness of my feelings. *What's Next?* took me on a journey of self-discovery at this stage in my life. I learned a lot about dealing with my grief. Bill's book was like having a personal therapist.

As a business consultant and leadership coach with a master's degree in psychology, I can attest that the neuroscience Bill uses to anchor his writing is solid. The exercises and tips Bill suggests are extremely useful, each of which has a story that enables the reader to internalize a 'life lesson.' Many of his stories are personal, which adds to the intimacy of the book. I strongly recommend this book to people of every age who want to improve the quality of their life, their relationships, and their success in the world."

—Tom Drucker, MA, ABD, founder and Managing Partner, Consultants in Corporate Innovation

WHAT'S NEXT?

WHAT'S NEXT?

How to Make Your Next Chapter Your Best Chapter

Bill Leider

Oxeon Publishing
http://www.oxeonpublishing.com

Quantity sales. Special discounts are available on quantity purchases by corporations, associations, and others. For details, contact the "Special Sales Department" at the address above.

Orders by US trade bookstores and wholesalers. Please contact BCH: (800) 431-1579 or visit www.bookch.com for details.

Printed in the United States of America

Cataloging-in-Publication Data
Names: Leider, Bill, author.
Title: What's next ? How to make your next chapter your best chapter / Bill Leider.
Description: Includes index. | Manhattan Beach, CA: Oxeon Publishing, 2025.
Identifiers: LCCN: 2025901483 | ISBN: 978-1-966550-10-5 (paperback) | 978-1-966550-12-9 (ebook)
Subjects: LCSH Self-actualization (Psychology) | Conduct of life. | Success—Psychological aspects. | Change. | Happiness. | Self-help. | BISAC SELF-HELP / Personal Growth / Happiness | SELF-HELP / Personal Growth / Success | SELF-HELP / Self Management / General
Classification: LCC BF637.S8 .L45 2025 | DDC 158—dc23

First Edition

29 28 27 26 25 10 9 8 7 6 5 4 3 2 1

CONTENTS

FOREWORD

In *What's Next?* Bill Leider skillfully weaves together neuroscience and personal development, offering a profound exploration of setting and following personal values while remaining aware of our blind spots. By incorporating the latest findings in neuroscience, Bill sheds light on the brain's remarkable ability for neuroplasticity, emphasizing how our neural pathways can adapt and rewire in response to new experiences and learning.

Within these pages, Bill delves into the role of the amygdala, highlighting its significance in regulating emotions and influencing our responses to external stimuli. By unpacking the workings of the brain's reward system using real-world and personal vignettes, Bill invites readers to understand how this primal part of the brain can impact our emotional reactions and decision-making processes.

More importantly, he incisively underscores the importance of leveraging our prefrontal lobes, the seat of rational thinking and emotional regulation, to make peace with our deepest fears and anxieties. By learning about the practical strategies and mindfulness techniques outlined in this book, readers will feel empowered to engage their prefrontal lobes, manage their emotions, and cultivate a sense of inner balance and resilience.

By bridging the gap between neuroscience and personal growth, *What's Next?* offers readers a comprehensive guide to navigating their inner landscape, fostering self-awareness, and unlocking their full potential. Bill's unique blend of scientific insights, personal anecdotes, and reflective exercises provides a roadmap for individuals seeking to enhance their journey on this earth by increasing their self-reflection and emotional intelligence, confronting their fears, and embarking on a journey of self-discovery and personal transformation.

Amir Vokshoor, MD, FAANS
Chief of surgery, Providence Saint John's Health Center
Founder, Neurosurgical Spine Group
Founder and CEO, Institute of Neuro Innovation

INTRODUCTION

Experience is simply the name we give our mistakes.

—Oscar Wilde

I have a lot of experience to share with you. I recently came across this proverb: "The tongue of experience holds the most truth." My own path illustrates the validity of that proverb.

Years of making and correcting mistakes, enduring the process of unlearning what did not work, reframing dysfunctional perspectives about what I believed to be my realities so that I could learn and act in far more productive ways—these experiences guided me to craft this book. *What's Next?* is designed to provide you a way to navigate change and embrace new chapters in your life that don't replicate what was but rather help and inspire you to lay the foundation for an uncertain next chapter in your life.

This book is designed to give you clarity, focus, and purpose. It will stimulate your curiosity to explore previously unseen, even unimagined, possibilities. Your path may reveal your potential that is different from your current state of being. You will undergo change.

Change almost always produces some level of fear-based angst. Ever since we became modern humans 300,000 years ago, our brains have been hardwired to resist change. In the distant past, we needed to resist change to ensure that our species survived. You will read about how that hardwiring operates today and how it impacts our decision-making.

That unconscious fear of change will forever remain in your thoughts, but you can consciously override fear and replace it with knowledge, certainty, and curiosity.

The knowledge you will gain will be a deeper understanding of who you are, of the capabilities you possess that will take you beyond your self-limiting beliefs, and of the strong foundation you will build.

The certainty relates to the confidence you will feel in the soundness of your exploration, the belief that your process will lead you to the place and space you want to be. A specific, fully defined absolute, however, is unpredictable. Scientists and philosophers have assured us that we cannot forecast the future, we can only imagine it. That is why you must believe the process will work.

Once you have acquired knowledge and certainty, curiosity emerges and overrides fear. Curiosity opens doors that lead you to explore previously unimagined paths, reignites passions you filed away in your unconscious mind as unachievable fantasies, and connects you with people who offer ideas you never considered. You will welcome surprises. You will consciously override your resistance to change.

When you replace stress with belief and curiosity, you contribute to your brain's health.

Change, and the growth you can experience from making change, seldom comes knocking on your door. You must seek and find your path. To do that, you must understand the process, the elements that make up the process, and the tools and skills you'll need to engage in the process, and this book will be your guide.

These elements will contribute to your learning, skill building, and active participation on your journey. As you read you will gain the following knowledge:

- How our brains progressed in their structure and behavior from the time modern humans first appeared on earth up to today. Understanding that will help you adapt to modern life.
- How instinctive behaviors that, in ancient times, served to protect us from danger today often lead to irrational decisions and stunted growth. You will learn how to prevent those primitive instincts from controlling you and how to replace them with wiser decisions and more productive actions.
- How to effectively use two tools that can help you experience a more rewarding period of growth than you ever have imagined. You will be able to overcome your self-limiting beliefs about what is possible for you to achieve and to be.
- How to create your vision, define your values, and understand your greater purpose. Those three elements form the foundation that will enable you to explore with confidence, clarity, and healthy curiosity.
- How and why those three elements must align with one another and how, if they do not, your actions will work at cross-purposes and keep you from achieving your goals.
- How to put all of this understanding and these tools together, and in doing so, how to chart your path to your gratifying next chapter. You just might discover that your years ahead will be the most rewarding years of your life.

I am not providing a formulaic recipe for an aspirational picture of your life transformed into an otherworldly fantasy about to come true. Rather, I offer you a process that will help you become more than you think you are. A self-limiting state of being defines most of us, but with this book, I intend to help you experience the joy of reaching your full potential. You will learn how to make the difference in this world that you were born to make.

The process you are about to learn is more complex than you might imagine. Alas, I am not offering you a read-the-content-and-check-the-boxes approach. As stated at the beginning, the antidote to angst is certainty, specifically one that is flexible. It is not cast in stone. As you read, you will learn to find opportunities that align with your vision, values, and greater purpose. Some will readily align with your preconceived ideas, while others will offer you possibilities you never imagined. I urge you to examine them all.

This certainty is spiritual. When you put yourself out there, announce your intentions, and have clarity about what you want your life to be about, you will uncover possibilities from previously unknown sources. You will feel opportunities speaking to you: "Pursue this, do this, master this."

You must examine your certainty within its proper context, which will shape the way you want your life to play out. For example, suppose you are an extraordinary dancer. Dancing defines the context within which the vast majority of your talent lies. Thus the genres from which you will choose—ballet, modern, hip-hop, or ballroom—define your content. If you are a ballet dancer, auditioning with a hip-hop group will likely be pointless, unless, of course, you wish to creatively combine the two genres.

Or say that you decide to be a full-time writer. Writing defines the context for your talent. But will you write fiction or nonfiction? And if you decide to write fiction, will you write science fiction, crime, historical fiction, or children's stories? Or will you turn to investigative journalism and write for a magazine? These elements of content all fall within the context of being a writer.

And for one more example, let's say you are passionate about health and wellness. You want your life to be about continuously learning and teaching others about the benefits of wellness, so wellness defines the context within which you want to engage. You have multiple areas to choose from. Do you want to specialize in yoga, meditation, acupuncture, weight training, cardio activities, nutrition, or a combination of some of them? Those areas of specialty define the content of what you will choose to do and be. They all fit within the context of wellness.

Back to your angst. For those of you whose trajectory in life has been traditional, around the age of fifty, angst may begin to creep into your consciousness. Many of you, however, may have experienced disruptive change, either existentially or self-created. You can experience angst at any age.

Considering or embarking on a career or lifestyle change can produce angst. Initially, you may not feel too worried, but when you begin to realize that your life is heading in a new direction in the foreseeable future, you are likely to say to yourself, "Things will change; I must change." Your angst increases.

Among the examples that supercharge this kind of change and angst are divorce, the death of a spouse or partner, a relocation from the city to a suburban or rural town, or graduation from college and entering the workforce without a clue as to what you want your career to be. Each of these changes, and many more, can produce angst.

How do you replace angst with positive anticipation? How do you imagine a future that is not an extension of your past? How and where do you search for something with a focus that eliminates the frustration of exploring possibilities that will lead you down dead-end alleys? That's a lot of questions and no clear answers.

But this book will help you uncover the questions and begin to find answers. As you progress by learning to develop your vision, affirm your values, and define your greater purpose, your angst will melt away. You will replace that angst with knowledge, confidence, and healthy curiosity about a future not yet formed but that you know awaits your discovery.

You are not a category or a data point. You are an individual, a distinct, unique human being. You have a gift that only you can deliver. At any time in your life that you choose or that unforeseen circumstances choose for you, you are capable of defining who you are and what you want on your terms.

To find your answers, all you need to know are what questions to ask, what avenues you need to explore to answer those questions, and a set of criteria to help you evaluate the possibilities so that you choose what is right for you.

I am not offering you a quick fix. Instead, I've created a guide to the work you must do that will enlighten you, stimulate your conscious mind, and help you adapt to changes that will enrich your life.

Let's get started.

CHAPTER ONE

HOW IT ALL BEGAN

The past can inform the present,
but it need not foretell the future.

—Anonymous

The story of values began approximately 300,000 years ago when modern humans first appeared on our planet. Since then, with all the inventions, discoveries, advances, and complexities in the way we live, one fact has remained unchanged: our brains are still wired as they have been since our beginnings.

Had you lived 300,000 years ago, you would not have considered having a vision, values, or a purpose beyond your desire for day-to-day survival. In those days, life revolved around staying alive and procreating. Death lurked around every corner. You would have been focused on finding food and shelter and hanging out with trusted tribe members.

To detect and navigate the perils of this hostile world and to stimulate a desire to increase the population, the human brain was wired with two instincts: (1) a desire for *instant gratification*, the short-term fulfillment of wants and needs, because being alive tomorrow was not a given, and (2) an *avoidance of discomfort*, because discomfort often predicted either serious injury or imminent death.

Both instincts are triggered in the amygdala, the small, almond-shaped cluster of neurons located deep in our brain's temporal lobe. The amygdala controls emotions and stores emotional memories of events we've experienced.

Our instinct for instant gratification produced a desire to procreate, which lives on today but has expanded to confront a vast array of choices involving tradeoffs between immediate rewards and the possibility of longer-term benefits of greater value.

The amygdala also triggers fear, a vital protective emotion. We make emotionally driven decisions faster than we do decisions that require thought and analysis. In ancient times, making a fast decision might spell the difference between living and dying, and the amygdala always played a critical role in ensuring that we stay alive—definitely more comfortable than dying. Making emotionally formed decisions also burns fewer calories than do those requiring thought and analysis, thereby keeping more calories in reserve to improve our ability to make better future decisions, again increasing our chances for survival.

Unlike our long-ago ancestors, today few of us face a daily risk of injury or death. We face different challenges, yet our brains remain hardwired with those original instinctive preferences.

Here's where challenges arise: although we cannot erase those hardwired default preferences—what we call our *instincts* or *human nature*—we must learn to override them. Those hardwired instincts influence our decisions and actions in ways similar to how our values influence us.

I call those two instincts *shadow values.* The big difference between instincts and values is this: instincts reside in our unconscious minds, and values live in our conscious minds. The difference determines whether we act instinctively or in a state of conscious awareness. Both states produce results in the same way, but acting with a conscious determination to live your stated values produces far better results. (In chapter 6, you will learn how to override your shadow values.)

Why Choose to Override

You may be wondering why you'd wish to override your shadow values. After all, what's wrong with instant gratification? Why would you want to give up ways of avoiding discomfort?

When you are under pressure, or when the pleasure within your reach is especially compelling, and you are not consciously aware of your values—especially ones that conflict with your instincts—your behavior will be driven by your shadow values.

Somewhere along the way, most of us learned that when we make decisions based on a desire for instant gratification or simply to avoid discomfort, in the long run we often get into trouble.

Envision, for instance, the way the actions listed below, driven in each instance by shadow values, almost always produce unintended, unwanted results:

- Instant gratification:
    - Eating a hot fudge sundae after committing to losing twenty-five pounds
    - Playing a video game until three in the morning the night before an early interview for a job you desperately want
    - Getting high on cocaine before a meeting designed to impress your friend, girlfriend, or boss
    - Having unprotected sex when the last thing on earth you want is a child
    - Buying clothes you don't need to ease your depression
- Avoidance of discomfort:
    - Marrying someone you don't love because you're the last of your friends who is single

- Deciding to have a baby because your parents long for a grandchild
- Not asking someone you like out for a date because you're sure they'll say no
- Coming up with every excuse you can imagine to avoid getting a colonoscopy, mammogram, or blood test
- Staying in a job you hate because the money is good

Over the course of your life, you likely have faced, and will continue to face, many such situations. In the throes of sexual passion, having drunk too many glasses of wine, nobody is thinking about raising a baby. But when a pregnancy occurs, you may ask yourself, "What was I thinking?" Marrying someone you don't love because all your friends are married may result in years of unhappiness and the emotional trauma of divorce, and you may wonder, "What was I thinking?"

Actually, you were *not* thinking, you were *feeling*. And while immersed in feeling, you likely acted on your shadow values. There's a good chance at least one of your conscious values might have helped you exercise the restraint required to avoid a life-altering mistake—for you and for others affected by your actions.

Shadow values often prompt regrettable decisions made solely to avoid the discomfort of change. Our resistance to change is pervasive in every area of our lives. All change is uncomfortable, so we invent a rationale to make our resistance seem logical, well-reasoned, and appropriate. With rare exceptions, these stories we tell ourselves are lies, designed to make us look good or hide our fear or both.

To resist change is to resist learning and growing. It's easy to see this resistance when we observe other people's behavior. It's painfully difficult to see it in ourselves. Some of us may see it but offer excuses: "This is who I am. I'm too old to change." That belief is simply untrue, a subject further explored in chapter 6.

One More Instinct

We also resist change because of another ancient instinct, our *tribal instinct*. Most of us feel safer being with people who look, talk, sound, behave, and believe the way we do. Such people usually feel more trustworthy and comfortable.

In our 300,000-years-ago selves, the drive to be among our tribe was normal and widely accepted. Today our resistance to being inclusive, to expanding our tribe, if you will, has become more nuanced.

A Story of Tribal Instincts

A woman had a flourishing career in management, and she was wholly absorbed in her work. Her primary outside interest was breeding, training, and showing dogs. She was a widow with two grown children.

One day she met a guy, fell in love, and got married (despite her sister's warning that such a thing would never happen).

She was lively, physically active, intensely involved in studying and applying nutrition and healthy living practices, an outstanding chef and baker, and an eerily good listener with empathy to spare.

Her husband loved his job and had no plans to retire, but she had decided to retire, and she looked forward to finding a few new friends and joining new groups, formal and informal. She figured doing so would be easy. She had always gotten along well with people. Besides, she wasn't looking for full-time activities, but simply meaningful relationships with women who had similar or compatible interests, shared values (respect, integrity, honesty, and no cheap gossip), authenticity (no superficiality), and an interest in what was going on in the world. She sought people with whom she could have meaningful conversations.

What she discovered was tribalistic rejection. Sometimes the rejection came with apologies that were transparently disingenuous. Sometimes it came with snobbish coldness. Some employed the newest social norm—ghosting.

Even for the most psychologically strong person, rejection can feel like a knife that cuts so cleanly, you barely feel it, at least at first. But even when that rejection does not detract from the rest of a full life, it leaves a cut.

Rejection left this woman—leaves most of us—asking questions such as, "What is wrong with me? What is it about me that is not good enough?" Even if the thought is fleeting, that wound is there.

The rejection she experienced became a topic of conversation with her husband.

I know this story because the woman is my wife, Arlene.

We both understood that the rejection Arlene experienced was living, breathing evidence of the way shadow values and tribal instincts often shape the trajectory of people's lives, lives led by a persistent resistance to change.

Arlene is not a moper. She looked at the situation as a problem to be solved. And because she is a great problem solver, sooner or later she will find solutions to overcome these rejections. When she does, her experience will trigger new discussions about how a few people were able to override their shadow values and tribal instincts to avoid discomfort and thus were able to experience growth through a new friendship.

For Arlene, this is a work in progress. Most of us are leading lives that are works in progress.

For those of you seeking to continue to grow and change—and you wouldn't be reading this book if you were not—understanding and overcoming the negative impact of tribal instincts is a vital step.

The Upside of Our Shadow Values

Of course, our shadow values may also serve us well. Some examples of activities where shifting mores that enable our shadow values to serve us include the following:

- *Shopping*—For millions of people, internet shopping offers the scope, ease, price and value comparisons, the quality ratings, and the ability to save time that make it an essential lifestyle choice. It can be gratifying and offer a new form of comfort. You might feel pangs of sympathy for small local merchants who cannot compete, but our needs are a worthy basis on which to justify achieving greater comfort and instant gratification.
- *Ridesharing*—The discomfort of driving and parking, especially in dense urban environments, can, for some, be eliminated by using a mobile app. Voilà, within minutes a car appears (with a driver, for now) and away you go. More comfortable—check. Instant satisfaction—check. Putting traditional cab drivers out of work? Regrettable but inevitable collateral damage.
- *Working remotely*—Remote work is complicated. The presumptive gains include more time with family and friends, less wear and tear on the car, lower gas and dry-cleaning costs, the ability to adapt and work with a schedule that can improve the quality of life, and the opportunity to live in a variety of places that are more affordable, have better schools, are safer, and have better recreational facilities. Potential losses include loss of human connection, decline in the quality of work, loss of collaborative opportunities, and a possible decrease in productivity. Is there less discomfort? Possibly. Less emotional satisfaction? Possibly. Again, our values come into play, and

to assess what is right for us, we need to ask ourselves questions about what is most important to us.

You now understand at least part of our evolutionary journey from birth to the present, from simple beginnings focused on survival to a world filled with complexities that grow over time. You also understand that while your shadow values will always be with you, you need not allow them to rule you.

Remember, your past can inform your present, but it need not foretell your future.

EXERCISE

Write your responses to the following prompts with pen and paper:

- Make a list of your current behavior patterns that align with one or both of your shadow values. *Be honest with yourself.* No one but you needs to see this list. It will be an important part of the framework to help you establish the values that will serve you as you move into the next chapter of your life.
- Write a list of three to six situations that bring back vivid memories of unintended results you experienced as the result of acting on your shadow values.
- Rewrite the history of those experiences by telling the story of what *would have* happened if you had chosen a different set of values to guide your actions.

Next up, you will learn two skills you need to create your vision, choose your values, and define your greater purpose with the wisdom and depth that will have you living life at your full potential.

CHAPTER TWO

THE MAGIC QUESTION

Accept your flaws in order to grow in your areas of weakness. Blind spots have been known to be dangerous from ancient days; let others help as they can see you better than you do by yourself.

—Dr. Lucas D. Shallua

What if by asking yourself one question you could free yourself of your self-limiting beliefs about what you can and cannot do? What if that question led you to see how your unconscious biases prevent you from seeing opportunities everywhere around you? And what if that question enabled you to envision possibilities beyond anything you ever thought you could achieve?

This question exists. Here it is:

What would it take to . . . ? Then simply add the issue you wish to resolve at the end of it.

I have posed this question many times in the context of consulting engagements and executive leadership positions. Offering this question always produced results beyond people's expectations. People's goals were ambitious. Here are a few of them:

- What would it take to increase sales at double our historic rate?
- What would it take to reduce our new product development time by 50 percent?
- What would it take to create a sustainable culture rich in diverse opinions?

I mention these business applications because over the twenty-five years of asking and answering this question for business purposes and achieving outstanding results, I never once considered the question as one that might address personal challenges—including my own romantic frustrations.

And then one day it struck me: how could I have overlooked such an obvious approach? Before I address that question, let me tell you a story.

One day in August 2008, hellbent on finding an emotionally strong romantic partner, I prowled the list of potential matches on an internet dating site. That day I connected with a woman who interested me.

The site required that we write to each other before meeting in person, and for a few weeks, we did just that. I found her attractive, and I guessed she felt the same. After three weeks of writing to each other, we made a date to meet for dinner.

On September 11, 2008, I arrived early at the restaurant we'd chosen so I could meet her in the waiting area.

Right on time, 6:00 p.m., she appeared in the doorway.

The moment I saw her—a moment indelibly etched in my mind—an internal voice shouted, "Oh God, please let it be her."

The moment we sat down, we began to talk. Within minutes, I felt this was no longer a date. We were two people connecting soul to soul. Time stood still. We were sitting in a dark restaurant on a warm evening, but I felt as if we were alone on a remote tropical island, beneath a cloudless, sunny sky, with nothing to interrupt the flow of our energy.

We stayed and talked for five hours. Our poor waiter was unhappy at losing a second seating. My generous tip didn't help much. But I was thrilled.

Throughout those hours, we talked about our respective values, our shared beliefs about life, and why meaningful relationships were important to us. Our beliefs and values aligned. As we were saying goodnight, we gently kissed. She told me she was leaving for a cruise with her sister in one week. She'd be away for two weeks.

I asked if she would like to get together again before she left or if she'd prefer to wait until she returned. Three days later we met for dinner. The following night, we met again. While she was on her cruise, we spoke every day. Our phone bills cost almost as much as the cruise.

Everything I learned about her deepened my affection and attraction for her. A widow with two grown children, she'd been single for twenty years. She worked as the operations manager of a radio station and had raised, trained, and shown Rottweilers. She'd once owned a home and ranch on five acres where, among other things, she owned and trained Arabian horses. She rode a Harley-Davidson, belonged to a Harley club, and rode in rallies across the country. She had purchased a small house in Manhattan Beach, California, then tore it down, and she served as the general contractor, building a new house on the lot. She'd done all this while still working full time. She trained for and ran half-marathons. She was also an incredible cook and pastry chef. Oh, and she had earned a brown belt in judo. I, on the other hand, was a management consultant, so we were evenly matched.

We discovered strange coincidences. When she gave birth to her two children, her obstetrician was my cousin. During our respective high school and college years (we both attended UCLA) we had lived within two miles of each other. For several years we'd hung out at the same restaurants.

Most miraculously, to me, Arlene was the strong, healthy, beautiful, accomplished lady I'd been looking for my whole life. And she was attracted to me.

When she returned from the cruise, we talked, as we had from the start, about the fact that we each were seeking a healthy relationship, but we agreed marriage was out of the question.

Five months and three days after our five-hour first date, on February 14, 2009, we married.

Ever since that day, Arlene and I have shared every thought, every anxiety, every fear, every thrill. We talk through our disagreements. We face every challenge together. We resolve any differences we have each night before we go to bed. Every day our love for each other grows stronger.

Sometimes we ask ourselves what we are doing wrong because people say all relationships require work, but since the day we met, our relationship has simply flowed. I am grateful for it every day.

But if this story reads like one about hitting the internet dating lottery, know that it is not, not by a long shot. The chapter of my life that led to meeting Arlene began sixteen years earlier.

Prelude to Magic

For decades prior to meeting Arlene, I unsuccessfully struggled to find a strong, capable woman who was attracted to me and to whom I was attracted. Nothing worked. The strong, capable women I met were not romantically attractive to me, nor was I to them.

My search for such a woman took a new direction when I signed up for a one-week personal development workshop being held at the Ritz-Carlton Hotel on the island of Kauai in Hawaii.

All my previous romantic relationships had been with emotionally needy women. My skills as a consultant and problem solver often became the foundation of the relationship. Once we resolved her issue, the romance faded. In fairness to those women, the relationship failings were largely due to my withdrawal. Without a problem to solve, I felt that I had nothing to bring to the relationship.

From initial attraction to failure, never once did I address the root causes of the failures. I simply blamed myself for making poor choices.

I came to the Kauai workshop believing that if I wished to resolve my issue—my inability to attract and be attractive to the woman of my dreams—I needed to learn how to make smarter choices.

Halfway through the week, the other ninety-nine participants and I were led through a guided meditation process. Each of us focused on our own challenge. That day, as my mind drifted into a meditative state, I found myself sitting on a bench at the top of a large indoor arena. Beside me sat an elderly bearded Asian man who explained to me that he was my spiritual guide and would answer any questions I might have.

In the center of the arena stood a warrior clad in armor. He held a shield in one hand and a sword in the other. All around the arena stood warriors in loincloths carrying bows and arrows. Suddenly they all began to shoot arrows at the warrior. I watched in awe as he either fended them off with his shield or the arrows bounced off his armor.

Suddenly, the action stopped. The armor-clad warrior removed his suit of armor and disappeared. In his place lay a tiny baby. The surrounding warriors resumed shooting their arrows at the defenseless baby, and many arrows penetrated the baby's body. But he never cried, and he did not die. Instead, as each arrow found its mark, the baby grew and grew until he became a strong young man with flowing blond hair.

Again, the action suddenly stopped. The blond warrior surveyed the arena and walked out into a sun-drenched morning. The surrounding warriors, walking single file, followed him.

I sat motionless, transfixed by this spectacle. My emotions were flowing—from my fear for the baby's safety to curiosity, then puzzlement. I turned to the guide beside me and asked, "What just happened? What does all of this mean? Am I just mindlessly hallucinating?"

"That baby is you," he said. "What you observed is what happens when a person allows himself to be vulnerable. Spears and arrows you believe will hurt you will actually help you grow."

He paused to allow me time to absorb his words before going on.

"You can remove your suit of armor without having to throw it away. You can store it somewhere. And if you choose to disguise your vulnerability, it will be there for you to wear again. Think carefully about what you have witnessed. It will change your life—if you allow it to."

As suddenly as he had appeared, my guide was gone, the arena vanished, and once again I was sitting in a chair in the workshop room. But something inside me felt different.

A few hours later, one of the trainers who knew me well from prior workshops invited me to join her in a private conversation. There I recounted my meditation experience.

She knew my relationship history. She knew of my desires. And she instantly understood my meditation. She told me my unwillingness to be vulnerable was the root cause of all my relationship challenges. She said that contrary to my beliefs, showing my vulnerability was a sign of strength.

I listened closely, but I felt uneasy. She was challenging my lifelong belief that vulnerability was a sign of weakness. I insisted she was wrong, I told her just because I wasn't vulnerable didn't mean that I was weak. She smiled and told me I was a coward. I dug in, becoming more and more defiant.

"Bill," she said calmly, "if you choose to do nothing about your unwillingness to be vulnerable, you'll still have a good life. You've said it yourself, you have a good career, a good reputation. You're enjoying a state of comfortable survival. But you will not have a relationship with the kind of woman you are seeking."

I listened, more out of respect than openness.

"Vulnerability is not a sign of weakness," she said. "It's a display of courage. That's what the baby showed you. It's the kind of courage that strong women find attractive. It epitomizes strength. It opens the door to real intimacy. It's sexy."

I nodded, but only to be polite. I didn't accept what she had said.

Two days later the workshop ended, and I flew home and resumed my normal routine. But a seed had been planted.

The Magic Question Emerges

That seed was vulnerability and my willingness to embrace it, to make it an observable part of me, and to feel it as a measure of strength—not a sign of weakness. When I was presented with that challenge, my instinctive response was "Not happening, no way."

But time passed, and somehow, with reflection, reason crept into my internal conversation. I was coming to grips with the reality of my results. Everything I had tried in the romance department had failed.

And so, months after that workshop, the first of many "What would it take" questions emerged: What would it take to abandon my belief that vulnerability represents weakness and replace it with a belief that my vulnerability is a symbol of my strength?

The belief that vulnerability represents weakness had been drummed into me from the earliest moments in my childhood. To answer the question, first I would have to reject my family's teachings about vulnerability. Those beliefs had not served me, but I had to find a way to reject the belief without rejecting the believers. I knew my family's intentions had been to protect me, not harm me.

Still, the logic of my realization did not ease the fear of thinking about giving up a lifelong belief. I grew up in a one-parent family. My parents divorced when I was seven, long before divorce was commonplace. My father left the scene. My mother and her siblings had lived through the Great Depression and World War II. With deprivation and war as their foundation, they lived only to survive. And they passed on to me their self-limiting beliefs and biases.

I emerged from my childhood and entered adulthood with my family's lessons etched into me, including the following:

- Showing vulnerability and fear were signs of weakness. Showing any of those emotions, under any circumstances, could be the death of me.
- Men must never cry. Crying showed weakness.
- Any level of success beyond mere survival was too dangerous even to think about. I was not good enough to strive for more than survival. In other words, I was not enough.
- In times of need, we have only ourselves to rely on, only ourselves to figure out how to proceed.

Yet despite these uninspiring beliefs, here I stood, a man who had had a great education from a leading university, a man who had excelled in both consulting and executive leadership positions. And while I'd long thought I could have aimed higher in business, my deepest belief was that I was not enough, which had restrained my ambition. Still, I enjoyed a comfortable life, but for that romantic void.

And here I was, staring into that void—my repeated failure to find my dream relationship. All these thoughts were the brew in which I spent countless hours stewing, reflecting. I relived parts of my long-buried past, reinterpreted my perceptions of long-ago events, and strove to look at them with a more positive, aspirational eye.

I thought about the ways my family had been deprived of certain financial comforts. For instance, we had never owned a car. And I thought about the ways this had taught me how to be creative and resourceful in getting around the streets of Chicago, about all my traveling via public transportation before I'd reached the tender age of ten.

Inevitably my days and weeks and months of reflecting led me to ask myself this pivotal question: "Was my willingness to show vulnerability the key to filling that void?" I knew there was only one way to find out.

Once I embraced that fact, accepting the changes I needed to make had been easier. My initial sadness, doused with a tinge of anger, quickly transformed into an awakening to the prospect of a fresh beginning, one filled with healthy possibilities. I could be vulnerable. I had the strength to accept that.

But now that I had the will, I realized I lacked the skill. I had no idea why, when, and how to show vulnerability, so my "What would it take" question began to take shape: What would it take to be appropriately vulnerable in ways that would make me appealing to emotionally strong women?

Like almost anything, there was just one answer: practice, practice, practice. I had no coach, no mentor, no role model. I would have to teach myself.

"Oy," I thought. "What horrors awaited me?"

And as expected, my initial endeavors were pathetic. I brimmed with questions that only experience could answer: What kind of person could I trust to accept a vulnerable me? How would I recognize such a woman? Should I display my vulnerability first and hope the woman would reciprocate?

These were kindergarten questions aimed at an adult audience, and I knew I would be clumsy. But I plowed ahead. I was determined to become vulnerable in an appealing way. And my new journey began.

I met a woman I liked, and after some months of dating, we decided to become exclusive—no dating others. A couple of weeks after we made that commitment, she told me she'd run into a former boyfriend, and he asked her to dinner on the following Saturday. She'd said yes. She told me we had to cancel our plans.

When I said, "That really hurts my feelings," she looked at me coldly and said, "What kind of baby are you? Grow up."

Our relationship ended that day.

On another occasion, while watching a movie with a date, when one character pointed a gun at another terrified character, I leaned over and whispered to my date, "That's how afraid I am of heights." She looked at me with a bewildered expression that seemed to ask, "Who the hell are you, and why are you telling me this?"

We didn't have a second date.

Along the way, I enjoyed a few dating relationships both of us knew were of a it's-fun-while-it-lasts-so-let's-just-enjoy-it caliber. I was able to show some vulnerability, but these didn't test my chops.

But the adventures continued for years. Repetitively practicing at showing my vulnerability became more comfortable, and after a while it even felt natural. My fears diminished. Alas, overcoming my fear of flying did not turn me into a pilot, and most of the women I met were not especially strong or self-reliant.

Throughout those years I did not obsess. I had a full, organized life. I had my work and my work friends. I had my tennis friends, my gym friends, my social friends, and my quiet time, which I treasured. I loved my house. I traveled.

Still, the ache of that void remained. When the pain surfaced, I used diversions—working more hours, playing more tennis, spending more time at the gym, watching more movies, and reading more books, knowing that the ache would eventually pass. And it did.

But it always returned, and I realized there had to be a missing piece inside of me. But what could it be?

One pleasant Sunday afternoon, while sitting quietly on my patio and reflecting, a sudden realization struck. For all those years following the workshop, I had looked at vulnerability only from the perspective of what I might compromise if I were vulnerable: my masculinity, my strength of character, my sense of myself, my self-confidence, my ability to lead, and my power (especially my power).

I had never considered what I might gain: greater belief in myself, not locking my emotions inside and thus producing a perpetual storm of unhealthy stress, having someone to share and help me solve my problems and allay my fears, greater intimacy, and someone who would see my warts yet still love me.

I could be imperfect and still worthy. The true me would be enough.

With a sense of renewed confidence, I began to see new possibilities. I could continue my search with a different energy. Three new "What would it take" questions surfaced:

- What would it take for me to consciously see and seek the gains I achieved by being vulnerable?
- What would it take for me to realize that vulnerability does not represent compromise?
- What would it take for me to focus on searching for a woman who wanted a meaningful relationship but did not *need* a man to solve her problems?

This is what I did to address those questions.

- In response to the first question, I became more discerning as I screened internet dating sites. I looked carefully at the profiles of women of interest, seeking to see where they were in their lives, their educational backgrounds, their desires for the future, what they were looking for in a potential partner, the ages of their children, and their interests beyond the superficial.

- In response to the second question, I needed to develop a better sense of any potential partner's feelings about the importance of mutual vulnerability. I could do that only through experience, and I made a commitment to engage in the process.
- The third question could be answered only through personal interactions. I had to become a better listener and ask better questions. And I also had to hear what was not being said. I committed to doing that. On paper this may sound clinical, mechanical, devoid of the lightheartedness and fun involved in discovering a warm, romantic relationship. But for me it felt fun. Blame my business background.

And as I moved on, my dates, whether one-and-done or those that led to mutual interest, all became more lighthearted and engaging than they had been.

Every experience was different. The women I met were different from those I'd previously dated. Even with those for whom I felt little physical attraction, the conversations were more interesting. I began to feel a sense of lightness and freedom, knowing I would not be called on to solve someone's problems.

In short, I learned what it took to be enough. It was not about my *doing* more. It was about my *being* more—more human, more willing to allow my partner to participate and share hopes and doubts and fears, more vulnerable.

My journey to becoming vulnerable and reaping vulnerability's rewards took many turns. I experienced painful times, exhilarating times, and always gratifying times. My pain fostered learning. My exhilaration was reason to celebrate progress. The gratification came with the knowledge that I was continuing to learn and grow.

And throughout these years, another deep, gnawing question persisted. What took me so long to see was how "What would it take" questions—those questions that had been so helpful to me and everyone I worked with in every realm of business—could help me to achieve my relationship goal. The answer was simple to understand but complex in its revelation.

I now know but did not know through those years about the way behavior patterns are established. Neuroscience researchers taught me that altering a behavior patten is difficult, takes a long time, and requires patience and tenacity.

Our most deeply held beliefs become part of our brain's survival mechanism. Even when misguided beliefs are contradicted by hard facts, common sense, and case studies with documented results, they can stick hard. I had spent a lifetime trapped in the belief that vulnerability was weakness, and even when proven false, the needle in my brain did not budge.

I had not seen the virtue of "What would it take" questions because until that workshop in Kauai and my many years of reflection, I hadn't seen lack of vulnerability as my issue. Instead, it was an ingrained part of who I was. That left nothing to question.

That firm belief in self-reliance layered on top of the belief that vulnerability was bad prevented me at that long-ago workshop from allowing the trainer's message to penetrate my emotional memory. I wasn't ready to accept the idea that my family's beliefs had not served me well.

I sometimes think that maybe, just maybe, the search took me all those years because I needed to wait until Arlene was ready. We'll never know.

I do know that in the end, all the pieces came together.

I dived into the deepest parts of me, to my buried past and parts long forgotten but still alive.

I dived, anticipating that my demons were waiting, ready to destroy my dreams.

But there were no demons.

Instead, I felt only soothing calmness.

I heard a gentle voice that told me to simply be the best version of me.

That's all. Just me.

Naked, like that little baby in the arena surrounded by warriors.

Vulnerable, always growing.

Improving my capacity for intimacy.

Assuring me that I was enough.

All of those "What would it take" questions and the process I used to address them coalesced and set the stage for the magical journey that began on September 11, 2008, and has continued every day since.

So what makes "What would it take" questions magic?

How do they work?

And how can you make them work for you?

What Makes the Magic Work

As Kurt Vonnegut wrote, "Science is magic that works."

Here is an important fact that you should know about the magic behind "What would it take" questions. There is no magic. Science is what makes the question work in powerful ways.

When you ask a "What would it take" question, elements of neuroscience and behavioral science are working in your brain to uncover previously unimagined possibilities. When you deeply examine those seemingly impossible possibilities, some of them will move from impossible to improbable, then from improbable to possibly possible. Once an idea becomes even remotely possible to achieve, you will have created a path that can take you beyond what you ever imagined.

It works like this. Nearly everyone has self-limiting beliefs. They are not true. Almost everyone can do and be more than they think they can. All of us have unconscious biases and self-limiting beliefs and biases that are not the result of some spiritual, preordained destiny that binds us to live that reality. Rather, they are our interpretations of the meanings from lifelong experiences, internalized in our minds.

Ego Alert

Enter your ego. Your ego's job is to protect you by protecting your self-image. Your self-image is framed by your self-limiting beliefs and unconscious biases. When you create a new thought, see a new opportunity, or are presented with a new challenge—and it doesn't fall within the framework of who you believe you are—your ego steps in and gives you multiple reasons to reject it: "You tried that before, it didn't work. That is not who you are. You're not capable of doing that." On and on.

Many people misinterpret the word *ego* to describe people with an outsized, overstated sense of who they are, their importance, and their level of ability—as in "He's an egomaniac." That level of a given person's ego is unbalanced. A normal, well-balanced ego helps people become confident, realistically self-aware, and ambitious. The description here of the ego's role is based on how a normal ego functions.

Your ego intervenes on a conscious level. It makes its presence felt in a region of your brain called the *prefrontal cortex*. That's the same region where you process new information, solve problems, and learn new stuff. It's also referred to as your *working brain*. How and at what level of intensity your ego acts depends on how new information or new questions are framed within your prefrontal cortex. A critical part of what your ego does—and how it prevents creative breakthroughs—is that it *judges* each thought, idea, and desire you might have and weighs it against an already formed concept of who and what you are. It rejects anything that conflicts with its preexisting picture of yourself.

Neuroscientists, psychiatrists, and psychologists have discovered that instilling creative, positive thinking while eliminating self-judgment from an individual's consciousness requires that the ego must be sufficiently quieted so it does not attempt to edit, judge, or prevent you from seeing or imagining anything that your mind can conjure—especially when those ideas are outside your self-limiting beliefs about what you can and cannot do or be.

The exact framing and wording of "What would it take" questions that you ask does exactly that. It quiets your ego at a level that eliminates prejudgment and diminishes your self-limiting beliefs and unconscious biases—especially when your thoughts fall outside the parameters of your self-perception.

The "What would it take" question is able to do that because it creates a blank canvas in your mind. When you ask the question, you don't yet know what it would take, so there is nothing for your ego to do. By remaining quiet (temporarily), your ego opens up a space in which you are able to play. Your mind is now free to go nuts with thoughts and ideas.

How might you feel? Imagine, for example, that ideas were money and you had carte blanche to spend any amount on anything you could dream up. Or you were a gifted artist, presented with a blank canvas and told to paint a picture of your destiny in any way that you could imagine.

When you ask "What would it take" questions in that context, many of your thoughts will likely be too wacky to consider. But you will uncover a few ideas that, with a few changes in your beliefs and behaviors and a little luck, just might work. Those are your golden nuggets. Those have the potential to produce life-changing results. Those deserve your time, attention, and commitment.

Depending on the depth and complexity of your "What would it take" questions, the steps you will need to take to achieve improbable results can be daunting. Almost always, your goal is worth the struggle. Almost always, you will discover that you are more capable than you believed you are. Almost always, you will identify areas of your life to explore that you had never considered.

In telling my story, I hope I have illustrated the depth, reflection, patience, and effort needed to make "What would it take" questions work when you address deep, complex issues. And as I stated in the previous chapter, my rewards far exceeded my efforts.

Next, I want to turn your attention to how you can make this question work for you in ways beyond what you might have imagined.

Using the Magic Question

Steve Jobs once said, "Your time is limited, so don't waste it living someone else's life. Don't be trapped by dogma—which is living with the results of other people's thinking. Don't let the noise of others' opinions drown out your own inner voice. And most important, have the courage to follow your heart and intuition."

You've read my story. You understand that the magic of the question is not magic, it's science. You understand how neuroscience works to stimulate your imagination.

It's your turn to ask "What would it take" questions that will help you imagine, define, and pursue ambitious possibilities, overcome challenges, and cast aside your self-limiting beliefs and your irrational biases.

Asking well-framed "What would it take" questions will release within you a refreshing sense of freedom to imagine the unimagined, shape the shapeless, and navigate the unnavigable. It can lead to reinvention—if you want it to.

The findings of neuroscience tell us that it is possible to rewire portions of your brain through a process called *neuroplasticity*.[1] Think about that. This means that over the course of time it is possible to reinvent yourself at any age. Rewiring requires significant effort, lots of repetitive practice, and becoming comfortable with the discomfort of sucking at your early endeavors until you begin to get it right and become proficient and natural in your new skin.

Asking and answering "What would it take" questions and reflecting, which we'll go over in chapter 4, are two vital skills that will immeasurably help you along the way. Think of this chapter, including its list of sample questions, later on as your user manual.

"What would it take" questions are ubiquitous. They can be used for any part of your life, from the simplest to the most complex situations. Here I focus the context and framework for "What would it take" questions to those aspects of your life that relate to your journey into your next chapter—creating your vision, defining (or redefining) your values, and determining your greater purpose.

A Big Question

Start with a big question that someone in any field of endeavor who is nearing retirement, or is already retired, might ask. This could be "What would it take to replace my angst about my future with a plan that has me focused, eager to imagine and explore new possibilities, and secure in my belief that I will find my way?"

You can take a question this broad and begin to break it down into a succession of more narrowly focused "What would it take" questions that will help you address the multiple challenges contained in the big question.

EXERCISE

Do this in writing, on paper. Do not type it. Writing by hand activates the left hemisphere of your brain—your creative self. You need to build that part of your brain to help you surface the memories that stir questions that strike at your core instead of dancing around the symptomatic edges.

Here is one scenario for breaking down your search and how you might form your question. Let's say I know that when I retire, I don't want to just sit around. I want to be involved in something that I'm passionate about. But what? Because of the nature of my work over the last ten years, I became stuck in my ways. That has carried over to my personal life. Going forward, it won't serve me well. I then ask myself "What would it take for me to become more curious than I have ever been?"

Then answer the question in writing. Here's one example of how that might look:

- What sources of information can I access to explore areas that I have never pursued but that might be interesting? What kind of people could I reach out to for the same purpose? How can I use social media to do both of those?
- What hobbies or areas of interest might I expand into a more fulfilling activity that would make a positive contribution to my world?

For another example, I knew a man who spent his spare time during his working career mentoring at-risk children from broken homes. When he retired, he created a scalable model for expanding that activity. He recruited other interested volunteers with appropriate skills, started a nonprofit organization, was able to find sponsor money, and found himself happily engaged in a spiritually fulfilling new post-retirement career. It was quite a departure from his life as a computer software sales representative.

Keep diving deeper in this exercise. Make certain that you have freed yourself from thinking only within the context of survival. If you are focusing on survival, you are still being held captive by your self-limiting beliefs. To overcome that, imagine something truly outlandish and write it down. It will help you unlock your imagination. Survival thinking kept me from expanding my own horizons for fifty years. Take the following steps to push past this thinking:

- List all the hobbies and interests you might want to investigate to see if and how they might lead you to feeling fulfilled and happy.
- Consider areas of potential interest that are new to you that you've never done or even considered but entice you.

  You'll also need to contextualize your list with your situation and goals:
- If you need to earn some money to supplement your retirement income, and you must keep that in mind as you explore your options.
- Maybe you want to travel to places you've never been. Consider if that could be included in your activities. if your travel be solely recreational.
- Or maybe you're a single parent. Your kids are grown and married and live far away. If you'd like to spend some time with them and your grandchildren, make sure that is part of your plan.

By doing this exercise, you'll have a list of things to consider—at least for a first pass. You'll need to play with this information. It will yield some real possibilities that are just beginning to emerge. This is the first step in an iterative process. With each new "What would it take" question, you must face every barrier you encounter with more "What would it take" questions.

Each iteration will move you closer to your goal of finding the path for your life's next chapter. Some of your most passionate dreams may seem impossible. They're not—as long as you keep asking "What would it take" questions and continue to find your answers. After a while, the impossible begins to feel possible, then probable, then doable.

More Sample Questions

You can pose "What would it take" questions that are broader in scope as another way to begin your process of exploration. Here are some examples.

- What would it take for me to leave my home and live in another state or another country?
- What would it take for me to give up my urban life and happily live in a small town?
- What would it take for me to see myself as more than an extension of what I currently do?
- What would it take for me to give up my need to please others so I can feel good about myself?
- What would it take to continue doing what I presently do outside the bounds of a corporate culture?
- What would it take for me to escape for a year and spend my time traveling and exploring without feeling guilty?

- What would it take to slow down and allow myself time to reflect?
- What would it take to incorporate living a healthier lifestyle on my newfound path? A number of good books talk exclusively to that.
- What would it take to reexamine my values and adopt new ones that better align with what I want to do in the future?
- What would it take for me to pursue my life's purpose instead of doing what my family and friends think I ought to do?

The Vital Role of Curiosity

Some people seem to be born with a curious nature. Others, not so much. If you are not naturally curious, don't worry. Being curious is a learnable skill. Seeing new situations, challenges, and possibilities through a "What would it take" lens will make you more curious (in part by helping you remove your self-limiting beliefs) and more willing to explore ideas that you might have instinctively rejected. Those rejections are the result of your brain's hardwired instinct to avoid discomfort. It is the voice of your 300,000-year-old cave dweller trying to help you survive. You can override it.

If you find yourself short of ideas, especially outrageous ones, force yourself to be curious. List ideas that you think sound crazy. For example, if you are a retired first-grade teacher, ask yourself, "What would it take to become an astronaut?" Nuts, right? But it might stimulate your curiosity about travel—something you have always wanted to do but were constrained by feeling you could not afford it. You are free to imagine the possibility of teaching under a variety of new circumstances. Your curiosity can serve to help you begin researching possibilities.

EXERCISE

Apply the "What would it take" approach to sticky or confusing situations you have faced in the past. Do this in writing—pen and paper, no computers. Note the outcomes, then write down the outcomes you might have achieved if you had asked and answered key "What would it take" questions.

For example, how might you have chosen a different course of action rather than taking a job that you thought you might hate? How could you have avoided wasting three, six, or twelve years of your life in a job you despised?

Or how did you allow yourself to get involved in a toxic relationship? What question might you have asked that would have led you in a healthier direction?

Getting Better at Asking the Magic Question

Routinely asking "What would it take" questions is a vital skill that you will need to own as you continue along your way. Keeping the following facts in mind is important as well:

- If you dig deep enough and for long enough, you will uncover your truths.
- Accept the fact that in the beginning, this will be a struggle. You'll sometimes feel utterly lost.
- Practice diligently, and you'll become good at whatever you set your mind on.
- Finding your passion is not enough. Once you've found it, you must develop the skills to master it. That's where the heavy lifting occurs and where the elation of achievement lives.

EXERCISE

To practice asking the right questions, take the following steps:

- As you go through your discovery process, write down your thoughts, your memories, and the beliefs you learned early in life. How have those beliefs served you well and how have they not? Doing this will set the stage for helping you form and practice new beliefs (your values) to better explore and discover during this next chapter of your life.
- For the next twenty-one days, ask and answer at least one "What would it take" question every day as you work to develop this habit and make it integral to your approach for discovering or uncovering life's opportunities and overcoming life's challenges.
- Take time to reflect. Get quiet. Go back in time. Examine the ways you acted on those beliefs that have carried you to your current state of being. Do this especially for those beliefs that are not serving you well. Use whatever surfaces through this reflection to inform the future you are creating. Write down what you learn.

I have just condensed what has taken me forty years to learn, apply and refine. Now you have it. Please do yourself an enormous favor—*use it.*

CHAPTER THREE

FRAMING THE MAGIC QUESTION

Clarity affords focus.

—Thomas Leonard

The single biggest requirement to make a "What would it take" question effective is to frame it properly. This requires understanding the root cause of the situation you seek to change, the problem you need to solve, or the opportunity you want to exploit and then framing the question within the proper context. Many of us are deficient at doing that.

To begin understanding how to frame your question, you must know three truths. First, all change must begin from within. You are in control and therefore responsible for knowing that to achieve understanding and acceptance, you almost always need to spend time reflecting. When you are attempting to change a current situation or need to solve a problem, first you must understand and accept responsibility for your part in creating the current reality. In other words, you must internalize the situation.

When you are reaching to exploit a new opportunity, you need to understand your role and how you will need to change as you move forward. Before you can address the role of others in your life, you must first address your own. When you resist looking within, know that one of your shadow values is at work, pushing you to avoid the discomfort of change. Tell your shadow value to shut up.

Second, you must become a central character in framing "What would it take" questions. If you focus your "What would it take" question on external events or on other people (as opposed to focusing internally), you will most likely fail to achieve your desired result. When you are not at least one of the central characters, and depending on the situation, there may be more than one central character, you are likely to frame the question around external issues. When you do this, you are giving up responsibility and control over possible solutions. Again, this happens when one of your shadow values convinces you to avoid the discomfort of making changes in your own behavior or beliefs.

The third truth is that reflection must become an integral component of change. This is especially true for change that involves abandoning preestablished habits, skills, and thoughts that no longer serve you. For reflection to become integral to your life, begin by using it to help you formulate and frame your "What would it take" questions. Reflection will lead you to the root cause of the issue before you, and as a result, it will help you effectively frame your questions. Reflection will lead you to take wiser, healthier, more meaningful steps going forward. Of course, one of your shadow values will likely attempt to intervene, telling you, "You don't need no stinking reflection; it's only going to make you uncomfortable." Ignore that voice.

Most of us want immediate answers and quick results, but in most instances, these either are not possible or not as helpful as we imagine they will be. Often, we abandon our search for the root cause of a problem that is facing us out of frustration. Giving in to frustration leads us to focus on symptoms. It's far easier to identify symptoms, quickly fix them, and celebrate our success than it is to identify root causes of situations we encounter. But if we address only symptoms, when the problem reoccurs later or when unintended repercussions manifest, we're simply back to square one.

In short, how well you frame your "What would it take" questions will heavily influence the results you will achieve. The key to success is your ability to address the core issue in your situation.

Alas, most of the time, our shadow values attempt to guide us to inaccurately identify the root cause. When we identify the symptom as the origin point, we may cure the symptom without solving the root problem. Long-term outcomes usually suffer.

To illustrate, let's say you have a headache. The brand of aspirin you took didn't relieve your headache. You might ask, "What would it take to get rid of my headache?" There's an easy solution, your friend tells you. Take two acetaminophen capsules every six hours for a day, and your headache will go away.

You take the pills. Your headache disappears. A week later it returns. Same remedy. Same result. Why did it return? You don't know. Your headache continues to recur. You keep taking the pills. Three months later your pain worsens. You finally go to a doctor, take a battery of tests, and learn that you have an inoperable brain tumor. If your tumor had been diagnosed three months earlier, it could have been surgically removed, and you would have been fine.

In the example of our fatal headache, a focus on the symptom led to the question, "What would it take to get rid of my headache?" Within the context of the question, the easy, quick answer—taking acetaminophen—made perfect sense. But the question never addressed the root cause. Focusing on the core issue to frame the question would have led to this question: "What would it take to determine the cause of my headache so that I can cure it once and for all?"

Asking that question goes to the core issue and also raises more "What would it take" questions: "What would it take to find the right doctor to address my headaches? What would it take for me to allocate the time needed to go to doctors' appointments to get the needed tests? What would it take for me to pay the cost of doing all that?"

But that shadow value urging you to take a few pills is so much easier, quicker, and cheaper. Alas, faster, easier, and cheaper might also prove fatal.

This truth is uncomfortable but because our brains prefer questions that lead to simple answers that use less energy, we are unconsciously biased to choose to address symptoms, stop thinking, and act fast. Our shadow values lead us to prefer instant gratification, avoiding the discomfort of having to think too much and of having our brains spend the energy needed to reflect.

The goal in this chapter is to help you to learn how to frame your "What would it take" questions to be focused on root causes and how to avoid being led astray by your hardwired shadow values.

Two common threads will guide you as one or both of these exist in almost every core issue. Once you have learned to follow the three steps above and you have identified which of the following two issues lies at the core of your problem, you will be able to effectively frame your "What would it take" question.

The two issues are (1) challenges that relate to the need for greater trust, and (2) challenges that relate to a shortage of resources, such as time, money, or talent (or all three). The following hypothetical examples will help you to better understand framing.

Example One: Anne

Anne, a writer, works for a youth educational organization. Her job is to curate and edit books written by the youth in the organization's programs. She is also tasked with promoting the work and designing and writing curricula. She is the only person in the organization who curates and edits the books. She works remotely as an independent contractor. She loves her job and her working arrangement. The organization has a staff of over one hundred people who work in various roles and a group of twelve who work for the program in which Anne is engaged. Most of those twelve people work on-site, at the organization's headquarters. Some work in other cities across the country. Anne has a one-year contract that will soon end. The need for her work is ongoing. She's doing an outstanding job with a track record of successful books produced and well received. Both Anne and Harold, the head of the organization, want to renew the contract for at least another year.

There is one major challenge. Anne wants greater autonomy in making creative decisions about the books. She is the only individual in the organization with the background, training, and experience in writing, editing, and publishing. She and Harold have had several discussions about her autonomy, but Anne is feeling frustrated, and her trust in Harold's leadership is waning.

While Anne welcomes Harold's feedback, her fading trust is the result of Harold's insistence that all members of the program team provide input on every creative decision. His rationale is that his approach is consistent with the organization's cultural norms, creates a greater sense of ownership by the entire team, and fosters a teamwork mindset and stronger staff support for every project.

On paper, Harold's rationale sounds good. He is focused on the value of cultural inclusiveness, but Anne feels this sounds better on paper than it plays out in action. As an artist with more publishing and writing experience than the rest of the team combined, Anne knows that receiving input on every aspect of a project, and particularly from people whose opinions outpace their skills, creates production delays, and more importantly, reduces the quality of the work. In technical business parlance, this kind of forced dysfunctional collaboration is often referred to as a *hot mess*. Yay team.

Anne seeks a "What would it take" approach to resolve this issue. Initially, in her frustration, she planned to ask, "What would it take to negotiate a new contract that would allow me to have the autonomy I need to do outstanding work while still satisfying the needs of the organization?"

Why is that the wrong question? The new contract referred to in Anne's question will be an outgrowth of the terms of a new agreement between Anne and the organization, a mere document. While Anne's needs are embedded in the question, the question does not offer a context for discussing those needs with Harold. For the question to be effective, Anne must reflect on and embed the core issue in her question. This will enable Harold and Anne to be on the same page as they begin negotiating.

The core issue that needs to be confronted is trust. Tension is increasing between Anne and Harold because of Anne's growing feelings of mistrust and her perception that Harold does not trust Anne's approach and solution because he believes it conflicts with an existing cultural norm. Anne senses that Harold fears a different way of working will erode teamwork, diminish group ownership of the books, and upset the camaraderie of the group.

Both Anne and Harold are being guided by their shadow values. Both are resisting because they are being directed by a need to avoid the discomfort of change and by their fears. Harold frames his discomfort in the context of cultural norms, which makes his position appear logical and in the best interests of the organization. But this is a classic example of fear clad in a velvet robe of good leadership. He fears the disintegration of the camaraderie he has worked so hard to establish, while Anne fears the final product will suffer if decisions are made by committee.

Anne's growing frustration is flustering her and making it difficult for her to frame a "What would it take" question to address both barriers—their fear and their lack of trust. Upon reflection, Anne has come to understand her part in this impasse and has come to a wiser, deeper question: "What would it take to structure my working agreement to allow me the authority and freedom I need to produce outstanding work that meets or exceeds our current standards, complete my work on time, and do it in a way that has everyone supporting it as strongly as they currently do?"

In this framing, Anne has addressed trust and fear without mentioning those exact words. Including staff support as part of the solution will reduce or eliminate Harold's discomfort and fears about working outside the organization's existing cultural norms. Anne and Harold are now positioned to focus their discussion entirely on both of their self-created barriers.

Depending on Harold's response, one approach that might dispel his fears is to pick a smaller, quicker project for a test run under Anne's proposed changes. Anne and Harold could mutually agree in advance that if Anne demonstrates under real-life conditions that her approach works as well or better than current practices, Harold will give Anne the authority and control she needs. If not, the current status will continue.

The sample question above is one of several possibilities. The important element in the dialogue between Anne and Harold is the focus on self-created barriers. As long as the focus remains on this core issue, the two will find a workable approach.

Here are the vital take-aways from this hypothetical example:

- If you ignore looking at the issues of fear and trust, you're likely to not address the root cause.
- When the issue involves two or more people, collaboration will always bring about a better, stronger solution.

Example Two: Pamela

Pamela worked her entire life as a civil rights lawyer and for the past many years as a lead attorney for a major nonprofit. She has since fully retired. Her two daughters are grown, and her husband is also retired. She has an active social life, a bevy of close friends, and enough money to travel.

Pamela has just one problem: her sister, Elena, lives nearby, is single, has no children and few friends, and does not work. Elena is almost entirely dependent on Pamela for friendship, activities, and companionship and most of all as a sounding board for her fears and complaints.

Pamela loves her sister, but she often feels burdened by her. Now that she does not have work as an excuse to keep her too busy to be at Elena's beck and call, she fears what is going to happen.

She needs to find a way to be a kind and loving sister but not get sucked down into Elena's sorrows. Pamela wants to make the most of her retirement years and to allow herself as much travel and as many activities as possible. She's had a hard time focusing on what's next because of her worries about Elena.

The straightforward "What would it take" question that Pamela might pose to resolve her dilemma could be "What would it take for me to live this next chapter of my life the way I want to, free of Elena's demands and needs, have Elena be okay emotionally, and maintain the love we feel for each other?"

Why is that the wrong question to ask? As stated, its sole purpose is to extricate Pamela from an unwanted burden, but Pamela is not recognizing or addressing the core issue—her complicity in helping create the problem. Even if Pamela were able to use this question to achieve her goal, Pamela and Elena's relationship is at risk of materially suffering and of perhaps being destroyed.

Several elements are in play in the relationship between Pamela and Elena. First, the extent of Elena's dependence has reached a stage in which Pamela is Elena's emotional support system, which is unhealthy for all parties. By not effectively addressing the core issue when it first emerged, Pamela has allowed that dependency to grow. Elena is exhibiting classic victim behavior because she can. Pamela's response—always being available and willing to serve Elena's needs—gave Elena the passive permission she needed to continue her behavior.

Since Pamela will be asking the "What would it take" question, Pamela must look within to determine the part of the problem she is responsible for creating.

Pamela must reflect on the circumstances that form the basis of her relationship with Elena to better understand the deep truths about why she has been unwilling to tell Elena what Elena needs to hear rather than what she wants to hear. Pamela will be more successful in restructuring her relationship with Elena if she addresses what she must change about herself.

In short, the internal must precede the external. Pamela should ask her first "What would it take" question about herself: "What would it take for me to tell Elena what she needs to hear about transforming our relationship to one of strong love rebuilt on a foundation of mutual independence?" Answering that question will help her confront and override her shadow value of avoiding discomfort.

Once Pamela has answered that question and feels ready to have the needed, challenging conversation with Elena, she can structure a "What would it take" question in a way that invites collaboration to answer it.

Pamela might ask Elena, "What would it take to have us collaborate to find a way to have you live a full, rich, enjoyable, independent life that does not require that I be involved in most of your decisions or your activities?"

This would enable Pamela to discuss with Elena the need for them to have a loving relationship as independent equals. She could openly tell Elena that she fears that since she is retired, her next chapter requires greater independence, and she does not want to grow to resent Elena and harm their relationship.

They might explore hiring a life coach for Elena. A good life coach could help Elena make wise choices and obviate the need for Pamela's involvement. With a coach's help, Elena could learn to trust herself, believe in herself, and love herself enough to be stronger and more self-reliant.

Depending on their resources, such a suggestion might generate another "What would it take" question, such as "What would it take to find and be able to pay for the right coach to help Elena trust and believe in herself." That kind of question falls into the category I described earlier in this chapter, the two issues that must be addressed. In this instance, the issue is the need to address a shortage of resources.

Here are the vital take-aways from this hypothetical example:

- When you ask your "What would it take" question you must first explore yourself to understand your part in creating the problem.
- The "What would it take" questions must connect with your need for trust and the resources required to address both the problem and its solution.
- Requiring collaboration to answer the question will bring about mutual ownership and thus will strengthen your commitment to resolve a problem.

Example Three: Stephen

Stephen is turning eighty, and although he is in good health and his mental acuity has never been stronger, he has begun to feel irrelevant. He notices that many people don't appear to care about what he has to say or what he thinks. Just five or six years ago he was still in high demand as a financial adviser and business consultant, but he has been retired for over a decade, and his former clients are also growing older. He feels his world becoming smaller and smaller intellectually, which is also physically confining. He is single, lives alone, and has not dated with any diligence or passion since he divorced two decades ago. Friends have urged him to try online dating, but the whole thing strikes him as absurd. The women he found were either too young or too old for him or too different culturally and intellectually. Most of his close friends are married or in serious partnerships, and although he enjoys all of them, and they usually include him in their social gatherings, increasingly he feels lonely and unsure about how to enhance his life. He has his hobbies: He loves to read. He gardens. And he serves on two important nonprofit boards. But lately life has felt too gray.

Stephen is searching for relevance. But his well-intentioned friends who are trying to help him are instead attempting to make him fit into their mold and their world. His friends' suggestions relate not to making Stephen more relevant but rather to having Stephen lead a life that mimics their own.

With reflection and a commitment to understanding his root cause, Stephen could come to understand that he felt relevant when he used his expertise to provide financial advice to clients who benefited from his knowledge and skills, and now, without these clients, he feels he has nothing of value to give.

Stephen uses the reasons he offers for rejecting dating as a cover story to hide his core truth: Stephen feels he has nothing to offer a woman or anyone else. Reading and gardening are things he does to please himself and occupy his time. They are activities that enable him to kill time until time kills him.

Stephen must find within himself a desire to learn new skills that he can offer to a new audience and that will provide value to recipients. Easier said than done.

His overarching question could be "What would it take for me to find a way to once again be relevant by doing something in which I find joy, passion, and purpose?" Stephen must think creatively, envisioning ways to provide value that are entirely new to him, things he never contemplated during his financial advisory days. To do this, Stephen must overcome a neuroscientific challenge. In his current state of feeling irrelevant, his brain is likely receiving a greater amount of the brain chemical cortisol, which acts to inhibit creativity.

Stephen's current state of mind is depriving him of the most important resource he needs to fully engage—an ability to think creatively. How can he climb out of this hole, fully engage his creativity, and find a path to regain his relevance and bring joy back into his life? Again, Stephen must address that question with deep reflection and a new point of view.

He must frame his challenge from the perspective of giving, not receiving. Unlike in his previous work when he received money for his services, in his new chapter, gratitude will be his payment. His earlier "What would it take" question might be modified to "What would it take for me to find a way to again be relevant by doing something in which I find joy, passion, and purpose, and for which I will be paid only by the gratitude of those I serve?"

Stephen's initial reflections might focus on the activities that he enjoys:

- What about reading and gardening brings him joy?
- At what age did he develop his interest in those activities?
- What factors contributed to his interest?
- Who helped him develop his interest?
- What is preventing him from delving deeper into those areas?
- Can either or both reading and gardening be combined in a way that will unearth his gift and lead to discovering his greater purpose?

As one example, Stephen might ask himself these questions:

- "What would it take for me to apply my love of reading to studying the health benefits of various herbs and vegetables?"
- "With my newfound knowledge, what would it take for me to use my gardening abilities to plant herbs and vegetables in my garden?"
- "By combining those two elements, what would it take for me to reach out to neighbors or people in underserved neighborhoods to teach them how to create their own gardens of health?"

The final question is the most pivotal one. To truly explore the possibility presented, Stephen must pursue his path to relevance by beginning as a novice. He must gain new knowledge about nutrition and growing healthy herbs and vegetables. During his working career (his former chapter), Stephen relied on his existing knowledge and skills to impart value and be seen as relevant by his clients. Now he will begin a new chapter with a little knowledge, a love for the subject matter, and a commitment to making it work. But he'll possess no deep reservoir of knowledge. He will be simultaneously learning and sharing.

Thus, his question becomes "What would it take for me to trust myself enough to learn and deliver the kind of value that will reestablish my relevance?" This scenario charts a new direction for Stephen in his next chapter. Taking the time to reflect and properly frame "What would it take" questions and putting his challenges and opportunities in this context does far more than merely helping him find something of interest in which to engage. He will undertake the process of reinventing the part of himself that made him relevant, and in doing so, he will progress from clumsy to adequate to good and ultimately to outstanding.

Neuroplasticity from repetitive practice will enable the change to become effective. Stephen's quest will be life-changing.

One of the important results of such a quest is the effect it will have on Stephen's brain health. Giving in the ways described reduces the amount of cortisol that Stephen's brain will receive. His creativity will improve. Experiencing the joy of giving will increase the amount of three important chemicals Stephen's brain will receive: dopamine, oxytocin, and serotonin. Those chemicals increase feelings of joy, euphoria, pleasure, connection, and trust with others. A pretty good happiness cocktail, I'd say.

This is but one possible scenario based on Stephen's areas of interest outside his prior working career. In this hypothetical scenario, the value to Stephen lies in helping him see and understand the way in which core issues may come to light and how "What would it take" questions can address those issues.

Here are the vital takeaways from this hypothetical example:

- When you are confronting the need for personal change, you must gain new insights to better understand who you are and how you became that person. Reflection is critical.
- When your next chapter suggests that you seek a direction and a purpose disconnected from your past, you must closely examine your interests, your passions, and the activities and interests that bring you joy.

Throughout my life, I have seen hundreds of solvable challenges in innumerable areas of life become sources of frustration, despair, and disruption simply because the issues involved were never properly framed.

The three most powerful tools I have seen and used are now yours. Effectively using them will change the trajectory of your life.

The tools are *framing*, to provide the right context; *reflecting*, to unearth the root cause; and wisely composing your "What would it take" questions using your insights from the first two steps.

By using these three tools with repetitive practice, over time you will excel. But be careful. You may find yourself getting calls at all hours from people you barely know to help solve their problems.

EXERCISE

To improve your skill in asking effective "What would it take" questions by using framing and reflecting, go through the following prompts, writing down your answers with pen and paper:

- Reflect on three significant, challenging past experiences in which you did not achieve the results you hoped for.
- Ask yourself how you could have reframed the challenge by taking greater personal responsibility for your part (the part over which you had control), and by doing so, how you could have reframed the challenge, asked a different question, and most likely achieved a better result.
- Reflect on the biases you held at the time of the incident that caused you to frame the issue as you did.
- Write about how and why your beliefs have evolved since those incidents occurred and what conscious steps you will commit to take to infuse your enlightened beliefs to productively construct your "What would it take" questions.

For example, maybe in your most recent job you were acknowledged for your hard work, but you were passed over for a promotion in favor of a fellow employee who had been employed for a far shorter time than you. To make matters worse, you had helped train that employee. You felt hurt and unfairly treated. You asked yourself, "What would it take to make my boss recognize my hard work and reward me with the promotion I feel I have earned?" You met with your boss and presented your case based on how hard you worked. She listened with empathy. Then she told you that, while she appreciated your position and understood your hurt, she remained steadfast in feeling that the other employee was more qualified for the promotion. You burned with anger. Three months later you resigned.

You spent time reflecting on your experience. You met with several of your friends and related your experience. You had a pity party, and the group concluded that your prior boss was a jerk and the company was unfair.

Then you talked to another friend. She had a different view. She gave you a perspective that shook you to your core and changed your life. She told you the world didn't work the way you thought it should. In real life, you are acknowledged for your efforts, but you are rewarded for your results. In reflecting on her words, you realized that since your early childhood you had lived your life believing that your efforts mattered more than anything else. Thanks, Mom and Dad. As you reflected further, you realized that you quit your last three jobs for the same reason—you felt unrecognized for your hard work. You never addressed the fact that, despite your strong work ethic, you often failed to achieve your part of the company's goals.

You revisited your history and saw that if you had framed your performance in the context of achieving results rather than simply *trying*, your work life would have been more rewarding. You would have experienced less stress, less anger, and greater satisfaction.

You commit to consciously framing your endeavors in the context of achieving results. You forgive your mom and dad for instilling in you a belief that, while well intended, did not serve you well.

Now, let us turn our attention to reflecting.

CHAPTER FOUR

REFLECTION

We do not learn from experience.
We learn from reflecting on experience.

—ATTRIBUTED TO JOHN DEWEY

The purpose of reflection is to provide a deep understanding of your experiences, the kind you need to build a solid foundation for growth.

Reflection will teach you about yourself in ways impossible to achieve through scattershot attempts at throwing words on a page and deluding yourself into thinking you are creating a story of substance. And by that, I mean a story that will open your eyes, ears, heart, and brain.

To build a serious foundation for your next chapter in life and to grow in ways that have you feeling focused, alive, and fulfilled, there's just one thing you must not do. *You must not do nothing.*

You also need these three qualities to help you experience the maximum benefits awaiting you:

- A willingness to look deeply and candidly at your beliefs
- Curiosity
- Faith that the true you is good

Reflection embodies art, science, and skill. The art of reflection speaks to your ability to see how you framed your perceptions of the events in your life that define your realities. Who you think you are is a montage constructed by your perceptions of the meanings of events in your life and the ways you applied those perceptions to other events. To see your perceptions in a new light, you must first understand how they came to be.

The science of reflection is the fundamental understanding of how your unconscious mind works to create your perceptions, how those perceptions are sent to your conscious mind, and how you have applied those perceptions to form your beliefs and dictate your behavior.

The skill of reflection lies in your ability to apply the art and science to reframe early life perceptions that have diminished your potential for achievement and growth. Enhancing this skill frees you to create a more constructive foundation, one better geared to help you become a more enlightened, relevant, and able version of yourself.

Through reflection we can reexamine our past through the lens of the present, we learn how and why we crafted our beliefs, and we reveal the interpretations and perceptions that formed the basis of our truths about reality.

Most of our early life perceptions are incorrect because we saw and conceived the meaning of our interpretations of events that formed our perceptions of reality through the mind of a child. The region of our brain that directs how we form our perceptions of what happened—our truths—is our prefrontal cortex. This part of the brain is responsible for activating our ability to reason, perceive, trigger appropriate emotions, develop attachments, plan, and solve problems. The prefrontal cortex develops more slowly than all the other regions in our brain and is not fully developed until we reach the age of twenty-five.

In the early life stages of development, a child's brain can see and interpret the meaning of events only through the lens of the need for love, connection, and instant gratification. A child's narrow, self-focused view—one not yet able to grasp the nuances, the peripheral consequences of events, or the many possible reasons for others' actions—will often create a sense of reality around truth that leaves us as adults seeing the world through the eyes of a young child.

Do you see a problem here? Good. Me too.

As we reflect, we are able to unpack all the nuances, the consequences, and the actions of others. We can cast aside our childhood perspectives and rewrite our story through a more enlightened, adult perspective. It will be the story of who we are and our full potential for being and achieving. This story will become our new perspective of reality. The findings of behavioral science and neuroscience confirm that doing this work is possible, constructive, and healthy.

The process of maturation unfolds like this: We live our lives with certainties, which are interpreted from the meaning of our perceptions, that form the foundation of our beliefs, our actions, and the results we experience. Within the context of that foundation, we adopt and act on the certainty of beliefs about what we are capable of achieving.

Most of our beliefs are self-limiting. Thus, we live lives of unfulfilled potential. And we are blind to that potential. This picture is wrong. We are wrong. There are no certainties. We have only perceptions of our experiences.

We remember and see these perceptions of events and people through the lens of our childhood interpretations and our acquired biases. Our biases describe what we want our stories to be, portraying ourselves in a light that justifies our shortcomings. We construct realities that help us feel a sense of belonging and acceptance by the people who are important to us.

Lying in our brain's database are events and memories best left unexamined, or so we believe. Recapturing those memories would be too painful and would yield nothing of value, or so we believe. The truths of our conduct would reveal us to be unworthy of respect and love, or so we believe.

None of those beliefs is true. What *is* true is that by reflecting deeply, with purpose and intention, we can reveal uplifting truths.

Counterintuition and Rewards of Reflection

Reflection is a counterintuitive process. Much of what we think is wrong is right, and much of what we think is right is wrong.

Reflection yields surprises. Courageously unearthing those surprises will make us more comfortable in our skins, more authentic, and more able to graciously accept life's rewards. Realizing that we are more than we think we are is one of those rewards.

Learning that freedom lies on the other side of the wall that imprisoned us with early life beliefs that no longer serve us is another reward. When we rewrite the underlying meaning of pivotal early life events, we are not distorting the truth but rather redefining ourselves by replacing childhood observations with broader, deeper, and more-informed adult perspectives. Thus, we are able to create a more enlightened version of ourselves, opening the possibility of attracting unimagined opportunities.

My Story of Reflection

In chapter 2, I told you the story of my journey to find the woman of my dreams. To reach my goal, I discovered, I needed to solve the mystery of my intractable unwillingness to become vulnerable. My logical mind understood the benefits of becoming vulnerable, but my emotional resistance overrode rational thinking. For years, I remained stuck in place.

Over those years, I reflected. Many times. Still, I discovered no revealing events until I summoned the courage to dig deep, diving back into my early childhood. This was a painful journey. I did not have the happiest early childhood in the world, and the thought of mining memories from that period made me feel like I would be ripping the scabs off covered but unhealed wounds.

I dived anyway. As I did, I began to recall, slowly and in no particular order, triggering events.

Our brains have two different memory regions: the hippocampus, which stores information about our experiences, and the amygdala, which stores our memories of the emotions we felt during those experiences. Those regions of our brains contain no calendar or clock connected to memories. Thus, as I dived, I remembered certain events and my emotions as if they had happened just yesterday instead of decades earlier.

I remembered bouncing along from childhood to adulthood with only blurred memories of my adolescence. Those memories had highlights—particularly playing sports (primarily tennis) over the continued criticism from my family, who believed that playing sports was for spoiled rich kids. They believed I should be working after school.

But I rebelled, and I played.

Not a single member of my family ever watched me participate in any of my sports activities. No one in the family ever discussed my athletic activities with each other or with me. From my teen years through my late fifties, I firmly believed that my mother had never supported me emotionally or motivationally.

And then one evening when I was in my midfifties, while I sat quietly at home hearing only the sound of the cascading water in the small fountain in my living room, a vivid memory surfaced. The memory was of an incident that took place when I was eight years old. On a cold, cloudy Chicago day in March, I was walking home from school alone. As I walked, two older boys from my school suddenly jumped out of an alley and attacked me. I fought like crazy, and although they ripped off my coat, I managed to escape and race home—minus my coat. When I calmed down enough to speak, I told my mother what had happened. I demanded that she go to the school and report everything.

She refused. She asked me what I had done to provoke the attack. Almost fifty years later, I could still feel the shock and anger I felt that day. She told me that she and I would keep this incident to ourselves. She insisted no one else must know. She said firmly that we would not speak about it again. I was to go back to school the next day and act as if nothing had happened, even when I ran into the two boys who attacked me. She seemed more upset by having to buy me a new coat than she was by my physical and emotional injuries.

I felt betrayed. If my mother loved me, I thought, how could she do that to me? At school, I became withdrawn. During recess I sat alone, refusing to participate in any games. In class, I stopped raising my hand to answer questions. I still did my homework and worked to get good grades, but I had changed. I was not depressed exactly. I simply felt alone. And I had no voice.

The passage of time worked its magic. My hurt dissipated. I buried my memory of the incident in the dark recesses of my mind with a Do Not Disturb sign tacked on it. But my anger and confusion persisted. A big part of me concluded that my mother cared for me more out of a sense of obligation than love.

Then, in my late fifties, while participating in a personal development workshop, I revisited that episode and its aftermath that had for so long remained indelibly vivid.

The trainer asked me if I had ever forgiven my mother. I answered firmly that I had not and that I probably never would. I asked why I should.

Later, as part of the workshop process, the trainer asked me to rewrite my story, with one new twist. I was to attribute my mother's motives as emanating from her love for me, from her desire to protect me from further harm.

My initial reaction was harsh and absolute. First, I dismissed my immediate urge to tell the trainer "Go screw yourself." Then I thought, "You want me to write some nonsense piece of fiction to make my mother look good. Sure, I can do that. But it will not change anything."

As I began to write, more memories popped into my mind. I reflected on my mother's family history and on stories I had heard about her father's fall from wealth during the Great Depression. I knew my mother had lived her life in fear. I remembered the lessons she taught me: "Keep your mouth shut and obey orders. Don't think you can be great because you can't. Keep a low profile, stay in the background. Live to survive, nothing more."

As memories bounced around in my head, I could, for the first time, relive my experience through mature eyes. My eight-year-old self was not able to do that.

A new perspective began to frame my understanding of the aftermath of that attack. While the events themselves didn't change, my interpretation of my mother's reasoning behind her behavior did change.

My mother, in her own way, I wrote, was trying to protect me from further harm. She reasoned that reporting the incident at school would put a target on my back and only inspire future attacks. I would be vulnerable. And I had no one at school who would protect me. She thought that maintaining silence would make the traumatic aftereffects subside more quickly. In her way, she behaved the way she did out of love.

Sure, my mother could have handled the situation differently. She could have that is, if she had been a product of a different set of realities. But she was who she was, and within that context, she did the best she could.

And so, fifty years after the incident, I was able to change my perspective of reality by recasting my past, which for so long I had interpreted through the rationale of an eight-year-old mind. When I interpreted the event from an adult perspective, forgiveness came quickly and easily.

Think about it. A memory that had tortured me for fifty years became, in a matter of a few hours, the impetus for my growth. Such is the power of reflection.

Following that workshop, other events from my early childhood emerged in my mind. As they did, I reframed the underlying reasons for my family's behavior. Reframing produced similar results. I was no longer held captive by the beliefs of a child with an undeveloped prefrontal cortex. All thanks to an understanding and application of the findings of neuroscience, I had a new and deeper understanding of my past.

The act of forgiveness, I discovered, lightened my spirit and freed me from the prison of the perceptions of an eight-year-old victim. Once free I was able to move forward along my path toward my ultimate goal—to allow myself to be vulnerable and discover the gifts that would bring.

Each chapter of this book offers suggestions for areas of your life on which to reflect. Please take yourself there. Some of your insights will confirm what you already believe in positive ways. Some will enable you to revise childhood perceptions and create a deeper, broader, wiser sense of reality.

EXERCISE

Do the following exercises in writing with pen and paper.

- Write about the areas of your life at any stage that have saddled you with beliefs, biases, and fears that have limited your ambitions, caused you to resist exploring new possibilities, or reduced your self-confidence. Set aside time to reflect about those areas. Only you can determine how much time and over what period of time you will need. I advise you to see reflection as a lifelong process. Be thorough. Go deep. The more you put into this process, the greater your gains will be.
- Redefine your perceptions of the meanings of your experiences in a context of you as an adult rather than you at the age when the event occurred. Use your adult perceptions to develop more enlightened beliefs as to the meaning of the events in ways that better serve you.

Reflection used well can be life changing. Practice it regularly, once a week, at a minimum. Its revelations will strengthen your new foundation. Reflection, in short, is one more element that will help you achieve unimagined results.

CHAPTER FIVE

VISION

We know what we are but know not what we may be.

—William Shakespeare

The quote from this epigraph is from *Hamlet*, written between 1599 and 1601. Ophelia's line (act 4, scene 5) was intended to arouse uncertainty and angst about the future. Unknown and unknowable events and conditions shape people in ways no one can foresee, nor for which they can plan. They cannot envision the future; they can only react.

Four hundred years of human experience and progress has elapsed since Ophelia first spoke those words. Yet today, many people live with the same kind of angst about the future. Fascinating. But it needn't be that way. Creating your vision will remove your angst and replace it with curiosity, anticipation, quiet excitement, and more.

Shakespeare's words handed us another gem. Interpreting and effectively applying his words, which were delivered in prose and grounded in neuroscience, can help you create a more meaningful vision, one that will enable you to bring to light possibilities beyond the limits of your current imagination. Shakespeare chose to use the word *may* instead of *can*. Note how different this line sounds: We know what we are but know not what we can be.

Many of us use the words *may* and *can* interchangeably. Think how often as a child you asked your parent for permission to do something. "Can I have a cookie?" "Can I borrow your car?" "Can I skip breakfast?" All are presented as a request for permission—to eat a cookie, drive the car, skip a meal.

Instead, replace the word *can* with *may* in your request for permission. Suppose you asked me, "May I climb Mount Everest?" In this construction you are asking me if I will allow you to climb the mountain. My answer will be yes or no.

If you said, "I *may* climb Mount Everest," I understand that climbing a mountain is just a possibility but not necessarily your intention.

If, however, you asked, "Can I climb Mount Everest?" and I don't know you, I might answer, "I have no idea. Can you?" But if I know you well, particularly your climbing skills, I might say, "Yes, you have the skills" or "No, I don't think you'll be able to do it." Either way, you did not ask for, nor did I give you, permission.

By now, you're probably wondering what any of this has to do with creating your vision. Patience, please. You'll soon understand.

First, you must escape the trap of interchanging the words *may* and *can*. When you begin to create your vision, you will be asking questions of yourself that address possibilities, desires, and capabilities. When you ask yourself those questions, you will frame them in specific ways and instinctively choose one of those words, *may* (or *might*) or *can*.

But your unconscious mind will process those two words differently. And based on that difference, your creative process will be altered. One of those words will help you unleash your imagination without roadblocks. The other will constrain your choices so that you are not exceeding your self-limiting beliefs. And your conscious mind will not know the difference.

When you state, "I *may*," you are giving yourself a blank canvas. *May* quiets your ego because there is nothing from which your ego must protect you. You are able to imagine anything without self-editing, judging your thoughts, or allowing your self-limiting beliefs and biases to prevent you from thinking about ideas that you never before allowed yourself to consider.

When you state, "I *can*," however, your unconscious mind will instantly restrict all your choices, making certain they fall neatly within the boundaries of your self-limiting beliefs and unconscious biases. Your ego will have exercised its power to protect you by operating within the bounds of your self-image. In doing that, you will also be aligning with one of your basic instincts—avoiding discomfort.

And it bears repeating: your conscious mind will not detect the difference between what *may* and *can* will bring forth. Remember, in the early stages of exploring possibilities. always use the word *may*:

"I *may* sail around the world."
"I *may* learn to speak French and move to France."
"I *may* open the clothing boutique I've always dreamed of."

If exploring requires you use the words *may* and *might*, when should you use the word *can*?

Moving Forward

Once you have determined the basic shape of your vision, everything you do to move you toward your vision invites you to use the word *can*, as in "Yes, I *can* do this or be this." This is especially true when those thoughts exceed your previously held self-limiting beliefs or conflict with your unconscious biases. You employ the word *can* as a motivating spark that ignites the action.

"Yes, I *can* open that boutique I've long dreamed of."
"Yes, I *can* raise the money I will need."
"Yes, I *can* find the location I want."

Remember, as you identify the "I *can*" challenges you'll face, you can apply the "What would it take" question to help you eliminate obstacles that might appear. I'll discuss that at length later in the book.

You still might be asking yourself why in the world I decided to use the words of Shakespeare as a foundation from which to deliver my message. I asked myself the same question. The answer provides us with another powerful force at work in the universe—one that will benefit you both in creating and pursuing your vision. That force is the movement of energy in the universe.

Scientists are still in the early stages of exploring and understanding all the ways in which energy moves. But almost every scientist agrees that energy does indeed move back and forth between the universe and our unconscious minds. It is happening, although we don't consciously know it.

In my case, here is what happened. I began to ponder deeply about how to illustrate your need to unleash your creative mind to give your imagination free rein to surface and explore unimagined possibilities as you create your vision. I want you to be free to put yourself on a path that maximizes your potential and opens you to what can become the most rewarding period of your life.

But as I contemplated, I realized I did not want to regurgitate clichés most of you have heard or read ad nauseum. My pondering produced nothing original, until one night, just before climbing into bed, I wrote a request to my unconscious mind. I asked for a new (to me) metaphorical connection that I could use to help people free their minds to help them creatively imagine their futures in ways they had never considered. Then I went to sleep.

The next morning, I woke and began my morning routine. Everything was normal. No flashing lights in my head signaling an epiphany. I ate breakfast, after which I began reading my emails. One of those inspiring quote sites that I see every day and mostly ignore featured a quotation that day that, for no obvious reason, I clicked on.

It read, "We know what we are but know not what we may be" from William Shakespeare.

I stopped. I thought about Shakespeare's words. I pondered their deeper meanings. Shakespeare, a master of nuance, expressed profound insights about the human condition. He raised pertinent, life-changing questions. He also generated questions by what he did not say. I applied all of that to what we're about here. You know the rest.

Then I kept pondering. How did Shakespeare's words end up in my email? The simple answer is coincidence, but I believe that is the wrong answer. The science-based answer, the answer I believe is correct, involves the movement of energy between the universe and our brains.

Our thoughts are a form of energy, a scientifically proven fact. Once formed, they don't simply rest in our heads. That energy is sent out into the universe. The universe is the receptacle for zillions of other thoughts zipping around at all times, the ultimate cloud storage system. When it receives a particular kind of energy message (for example, my request), it has the capability to match it with a compatible energy (Shakespeare's words) and send it back to the entity that made the request (my mind). Sometimes the connection is not obvious. Often the recipient must be ready to receive an answer that is not in a form anticipated when the request was made. This means we must always be consciously aware, alert, and adaptable.

You too have this source of energy available from which opportunities, ideas, and answers will appear. They will come to you in response to the thoughts you express and the requests you make—even when you don't have a clue as to the answers you are seeking. You need to remain consciously aware so you don't miss those answers.

Moving toward your vision is never a solo journey. In most cases it should not be a secret. Be transparent. Let the world know of your vision. Doing so will attract helpful people and useful resources. They will appear as if by magic. But it's not magic. It's how energy moves through the universe.

Forces at Play to Help You on Your Path

You now have three effective procedures to use as you create your vision:

- Address barriers and challenges you encounter with "What would it take" questions to overcome them.
- Use the words *may* or *might* to identify the most creative possibilities.
- Maintain constant, conscious awareness so you can make requests and receive answers that will from time to time appear from people and sources you never knew existed.

You, Me, and the Visionaries

Some peoples' visions have changed the world. They transcended the personal and engaged millions. They have unfolded over generations and lifetimes. Just as we don't know at the time of a baby's birth what that baby's lifetime experiences will be, those visionaries did not know the precise path and plan for achieving their visions at the times they created them.

Mother Teresa had a vision: to care for the poorest of the poor. Elie Wiesel, Holocaust survivor and Nobel Peace Prize winner, had a vision: to make the Holocaust a living memory, remembering for the future. Dr. Martin Luther King Jr. had a vision (he called it a dream): "That one day my four little children will live in a nation where they will not be judged by the color of their skin but by the content of their character."

Their visions shared some common threads. They each sought to create a better world. Each envisioned a future time and place beyond their lifetimes. None knew the path they would follow, the challenges they might face, and the measure of grit and resilience they would need to move toward their vision. But they all knew from the outset that their visions would need to attract and bring in thousands, even millions of people who would share and help achieve those visions.

I cite these three examples to demonstrate the power a vision can have. But a vision need not be grandiose. Every one of us can channel the same kind of power, scaled in scope, to achieve what we want our futures to be.

Creating Your Vision: The Beginning

To start creating your vision, here is a working definition you can use. Your vision is your dream about what you want your life to be, what you want to experience, what makes you feel alive and vibrant, and what fulfills you—at some point in the future. It contains the substance of what you want to experience, but it does not have a specific form or structure. You can see it in your mind's eye, but you do not yet know how to get there.

I want to focus on the kind of vision you will need as you navigate the next chapter of your life. You may be approaching the journey with some angst that cannot be quieted until you know what the hell you're going to be doing and are excited about getting started.

Angst is stressful. Positive certainty is comforting. You want to make that transformation yesterday. You might be saying to yourself, "Okay, enough with the narrative. Give me the answer—*now*."

That's not possible because if your vision is going to be meaningful and if it will guide you the way great visions do, you will not land on it quickly—even if you think you already have chosen some terrific goals for your future.

To begin, make angst your friend. Embrace it. Explore the feelings that fuel it. Congratulate yourself for experiencing it. Angst is the foundation for uncovering your options in the most meaningful way possible.

EXERCISE

As you discover the sources and their reasons for generating your angst, write them down. Writing them adds an element of depth and clarity that you need and that you will not remember unless you write about them.

Here are some examples:

- "I want to retire from my job but not from life. I want to do something meaningful with the rest of my life. I'd like to earn some money, but I don't need to be enslaved by money. What might that look like? I don't have a clue."
- "I'd like to live somewhere else. I'm tired of city congestion, rising crime, divisive politics, and increasing homelessness. But I've lived here all my life. I haven't traveled much. I have no idea where I might want to go. And I don't know how to find out. What can I do about this?"
- "I want travel to be a big part of my life. I need to incorporate some kind of activity that I enjoy and that I can earn some money from that will blend in with my travels. I don't have a clue what that could be. How do I find out?"
- "I just retired. Right now, I have no desire to do anything. I'm happy to spend my days reading, taking

walks, visiting friends, seeing more of my children and grandchildren, and puttering around my house. I have a feeling that at some point that won't be enough. I will get bored. Then what? I don't know, and that feeling of not knowing is already gnawing at me. How can I begin to plan for that time?"

All of the above serve to create the context within which you can bring your vision to life. Now it's your turn to dream, imagine, and create interesting pursuits. Do not edit or judge your thoughts. Just let them flow. Write them down. You have a blank canvas in front of you. There are no limits or rules as to what you can put on that canvas.

Here are some suggestions for questions to ask yourself:

- What have you always wished you could pursue before life got in the way?
- What would you do differently if you could erase time and live all over again?
- What talent do you have that you chose or were forced to abandon?
- How would you spend the rest of your days if money were not a problem? Don't be seduced by the allure of going on an endless number of cruises. All the people I have known who tried that were bored out of their minds after six months.
- What causes are you passionate about, and which ones would be fulfilling to volunteer your time to help?
- Where would you like to be living if it's different from where you live now?

- What kind of new friends do you want to attract?
- What attracts you when you think of making a difference in the world or in the lives of others?
- What do you want to get rid of?

You might see yourself doing something entirely different from what you currently do or living in a different place and adapting to a new lifestyle. You might spend most of your time traveling the world. Then again, you might be doing a version of what you currently do but with a different focus to a different audience. Or you might find a way to continue to do what you are now doing because it is your calling. You might turn your hobby into your passionate, full-time endeavor. Or you might package the knowledge you've gained throughout your life and find a vehicle to teach others valuable skills. You might see yourself going back to school, learning things you've often dreamed about but never pursued. And whatever else you can conjure up.

The list above is a sample to help you get started. You will have many more thoughts. Just give yourself permission to imagine with no boundaries. I repeat: put your thoughts and ideas in writing. This is very important.

Remember This

Doing this is more important as you contemplate and live this next chapter of your life because you don't have as much time to screw around with stuff that doesn't get you where you want to be, what you want, and why you want it. You want to get going.

When you see what you want, frame it, and feel it, you will have created your *vision*. Your vision is your future not yet manifest. It can be grand or modest. Its scope is yours to determine. You and only you have the right to decide.

Your vision can be achievable in your lifetime, or it can stretch to encompass generations to come. Your vision becomes your North Star, illuminating the path you will take to achieve it. Your vision also serves as your foundation. It becomes the guardrails that will keep you focused to pursue avenues and activities that align with it.

Your vision answers the question, "What may you be?" Once you've formed your vision, you will activate it by your actions over time.

My Story of Inherited Values

My mother lived in fear. When she was growing up, her father was wealthy. She led a life of privilege—until Tuesday, October 29, 1929 (Black Tuesday), the day the stock market crashed and the Great Depression began. My grandfather went from powerful to pauper in twenty-four hours, as did his children.

He never recovered. Emotionally, neither did my mother. My grandfather died when I was twelve. He was poor but proud. I never really knew him. I never got to hear him tell his story. I was at the mercy of my mother's interpretation of the meaning of the experience.

She passed her interpretation on to me in the form of advice about how to live. As a child, a teenager, and a young adult, I did not understand the basis of her beliefs. I knew only the content of her message. It went like this: When you grow up and go out into the world, keep a low profile. Do as you're told. Don't talk back. Don't resist. Obey orders. Survive. That's as good as you can expect. Don't ever think that you're anything special or talented because you're not. Don't get any big ideas about standing out.

As damaging as that sounds, I eventually learned that she gave me those messages to protect me from the fate that befell her father. She did not want that to happen to me.

During my college days and early in my career, I had a number of successful experiences that told me my mother's message was not serving me well. In my senior year at UCLA, I made the dean's list. Early in my career, I landed a position at one of the premier boutique accounting firms in the country. When I chose to leave the world of public accounting, I became the chief financial officer of the second largest auto glass distribution company in the country at the age of twenty-seven. Yet I ignored all those positive messages. In my mind I believed I was not enough.

The result was that my only goal in my business life and personal life was to *comfortably survive*—one day at a time, one encounter at a time. Keep my head down and don't think about anything beyond the immediate present and whatever life served up.

Yet as blind to opportunities and long-range goals as I was, I never saw myself as a victim. I was comfortably surviving. I was a good provider but not as sensitive and demonstratively loving a father as I should have been. I was too busy and buried in maintaining comfortable survival to look around. Even a broken marriage wasn't a sufficient wake-up call to force me to examine my fundamental beliefs. It's shameful—and human.

It has taken me a long time and a lot of work to forgive myself and to forgive and understand my mother.

That describes the first fifty years of my life. Only then did I begin in earnest to study change and reflect deeply about who I was, who I wanted to become, how to begin that journey, and what I wanted the rest of my life to be about.

When I talk about the importance of having a vision and the harm of not having one, I am speaking as someone who has experienced both. Scientific research and studies are important for understanding people in a statistical sense. But I am not speaking to you as a statistic or a data point. This is *me* talking to *you* through the lens of my experience. That future time could be as soon as next year and it could be as far away as years or decades beyond your life expectancy. That vision can depict something specific and measurable. For example,

> I have a vision that two years from today I will be living in a beautiful home and studio overlooking the sea. I will still be working as a graphic artist, but I will work from home. My accomplishments and reputation will enable me to have as much work and as much free time as I want. I will spend three months of the year traveling to places I've never been.

Or it can be amorphous as to time and shape. For example,

> Through my creative ideas, brought to life in the field of graphic arts, my work will expand the power of this art form and forge new frontiers in the ways people see and experience graphic images. All of society will benefit.

The Flavors

Throughout my business career and based on everything I've experienced, read about, and studied, visions take on one of three flavors. One depicts a future that describes an enhanced version of who you already are, doing what you're currently doing but better. The second envisions a future reality that does not connect to what you currently do or who you perceive yourself to be. It is less specific and more amorphous and opens doors to currently unimagined possibilities. The third is a combination of the first two. You imagine yourself being and doing what you currently do. At the same time, you envision breaking new ground, discovering something entirely different and making it part of the new you.

In our personal lives, our brains work the same way. Your vision will most likely take on one of these three forms. For example, in version one, let's say you have been a schoolteacher for your entire working life. You have either retired or are preparing for retirement. You love teaching and want to continue to teach for as long as your physical and mental health make it possible. During your career, you primarily taught high school history. Curriculum standards constrained you from making history as exciting as you know it can be. You wanted to bring in more stories, expand the curriculum to include relevant new literature, and dive deeper into the cultural and political norms that shaped events.

Free of constraints, your vision might sound like this:

> I will find a teaching opportunity that expands my love of history, free of the bureaucratic constraints that have held me back. The environment in which I teach will be open, nurturing, and focused on delivering an elevated level of learning that young minds will embrace and use to create a better world.

This vision describes an enhanced version of who you are.

In the second version, you are that same teacher. While you still enjoy teaching, you're burned out. You want an active, vibrant life but not necessarily one designed around teaching. You love traveling—globally, archaeology, and writing. You could see yourself living in another country doing any combination of the activities you love. But what would that look like? You have no clue. And you shouldn't—not at this stage.

Your vision might sound like this:

> I will experiment to find outlets for my passions. I will expand my awareness of the possibilities that await me. I will be open-minded, creative, and attuned to opportunities beyond anything I have imagined. And I will find an exciting opportunity that will allow me to be the version of myself that I have longed for.

Yours will be a vision that involves reinventing who you are.

In the third version, you are that same teacher. You still love teaching and would like to continue to teach but not in the same place. You love to travel domestically, and your hobby has been photography. You're a good photographer and like to focus on historic structures. If only there were an opportunity out there that would enable you to do all of those things as a part of your new endeavor. It is there, waiting for you. You just need to discover it. You don't know what that opportunity might look like or where to find it, but that is the perfect place from which to begin.

Your vision might sound like this:

> I will discover a unique opportunity that enables me to combine my teaching experience with my skill in photographing historically significant structures around the country. It will allow me to interpret and teach history with an added dimension that is unique. It will be fulfilling for me and enriching for those I teach. I don't know what it looks like today, but I will search diligently, and I will know it when I find it.

This vision takes what you already do and adds a dimension that enriches your experience, your satisfaction, and your ability to make a difference in the world.

All three versions of a vision have two things in common. First, they talk to a future reality not yet manifest. Second, you don't know how you will get there.

At the time you create your vision, it is a dream—your dream. You must *capture that dream in writing*. Doing so gives it a sense of realizable possibility. It is your future. It simultaneously becomes a North Star to guide you and the foundation for the path you will take to get there.

In all likelihood, when you write it down for the first time, you will not create a clear picture. How could you? You are envisioning something you've never experienced. Be patient. You are creating a verbal picture of your future life. It should take several attempts. The process could take weeks, even months. That is as it should be.

What will finally appear is a picture, created in words, that you can see and embrace. Keeping it in mind will help you avoid the distractions that take you off track. You now have a path that you can use to create your future. You may never fully achieve your whole vision. And that is what makes a vision so relevant. Because while you may never get all the way there, your vision's presence is your constant North Star for finding clarity, direction, and focus.

When you come across an interesting person or an opportunity that seems inconsistent with your vision, stop and ask yourself, "Is this taking me toward my vision or away from it? If it's taking me away, why am I allowing this to happen? And if I'm allowing it to happen, what would it take for me to get back on the path to my vision?"

Brain Fog Alert

You might attempt this process and discover that nothing bubbles up. The blank sheet of paper you started with remains blank. You might be thinking, "This process sucks. I don't know what I'm talking about. I don't know what I'm doing. This is crazy."

Don't give up. The reason you're having trouble putting words down on the page is that you are unconsciously editing and judging your thoughts. And after having done so, you're rejecting them.

To overcome that block, ask yourself the magic question, and ask with genuine intent: "What would it take to imagine having everything in life that I've ever dreamed of wanting and writing it down without editing my thoughts?"

As your vision becomes visible, it begins to become realizable. And as you begin to see yourself moving in its direction, continue to refine it as you see fit.

Your vision is not yet set in stone. Your next step will be to examine your values, modify them based on your current beliefs, and make certain that your vision aligns with those values and your greater purpose (discussed in depth in chapter 7). The alignment of those three elements is the only way to ensure that your conduct, your choices, and the energy that you emit and attract will all work in harmony to optimize the quality of your life.

For now, let your vision rest a bit, and we'll turn our attention to your values.

CHAPTER SIX

VALUES

To thine own self be true.

—WILLIAM SHAKESPEARE

Values. Misunderstood by many, consciously and consistently adhered to by few, values live in the shadows of our conscious minds, summoned to help guide us, primarily in times of crisis.

Due to their limited use, your values remain a source of untapped potential that, if properly applied, can immeasurably help you live a more rewarding life.

What Exactly Are Values?

Our values are our unconditional beliefs about how we commit to live, demonstrated and made credible by our consistent conduct over time.

The way in which you live your values becomes the lens through which others see, understand, and judge you. Your behavior is the evidence—your values in action—that defines you to others and to yourself. Your behavior also affects the kind of energy you emit and receive. It determines the people you attract and those you repel. It influences the outcomes of your endeavors in every area of your life.

Many people are confused about the precise meaning and application of values. Throughout your life you've likely had encounters with American values, religious or spiritual values, personal values, corporate values, and situational values. Each of those sets of values contains elements of the definition above. Each presents values as guides, influences, suggestions, or desired (but not required) beliefs. All of them place values in the shadows of your everyday consciousness. You probably don't think about your values in your day-to-day conduct—most of us don't.

The categories listed above and their applications do not hit the nail on the head.

You likely believe—most of us do—that the values your family taught you when you were young are indelibly etched into your brain and carved into your heart. You likely believe they are yours for life, that they define you, and that you cannot change them—which naturally limits the ways you can change yourself.

Think again. Scientific research has proven this prevalent belief to be a myth. You can change your values at any time in your life if you decide and commit to doing so. You may, for example, discover that some of your values are not serving you. You may, like me, learn over time that values you learned early in life and accepted as absolute led you to frustration and failure when it came to achieving your goals.

The good news is this: with repetitive practice, through a process called *neuroplasticity*, you can rewire your brain and learn new habits, behaviors, and values. You are not condemned to be imprisoned by your past.

This chapter offers you the most rigorous and perhaps the least enjoyable challenge yet. Determining and defining your current values and deciding what your values will be going forward may be difficult. But it is critically important and, I promise, most rewarding.

So hang in there and follow me step by step. Your effort will prove worthwhile.

Step One: Thinking about and Understanding Your Values

First, cast aside all the depictions of the various interpretations of values. Cast aside your religious and spiritual values, your country-of-origin values, your corporate values, and your situational and family values.

We are about to focus on *your* values. These will become your guide and commitments. And when you align them with your vision and your greater purpose, you will propel yourself to new heights.

Remember the definition from earlier: our values are our unconditional beliefs about how we commit to live, demonstrated and made credible by our consistent conduct over time. Two words in this definition deepen and differentiate their true strength: *unconditional* and *commit.*

Unconditional, in the context of your values, means that you cannot behave situationally or conditionally. You must live your values no matter the situation or other peoples' conduct or expectations.

For example, you cannot claim respect as your value but respect only those who respect you in return. You cannot respect only people you like or people with whom you agree on important topics or people whose lifestyle you deem acceptable.

This can be challenging. Why, you may wonder, would you respect someone who does not respect you? Or someone whose worldview is diametrically opposite to yours? Or a drug addict who defecates on your front lawn?

The easy answer is this: you don't have to. But if you don't, can't, or won't, you must acknowledge that respect is not one of your values. Instead, understand that respect is your conditional choice based on circumstances and on your judgment as to whether another person deserves your respect.

If, though, respect is one of your core values, you must rise above another's conduct or the situation that you deem to be disrespectful of you. You must look at others from a higher level. You may condemn the act, but you may not condemn the actor.

This does not mean that bad deeds must go unpunished. You may disagree with others yet respect their right to exist and to hold their beliefs. For example, you can respect someone's right to hold misogynistic views toward women, but you likely won't show up at the person's weekend barbeque. You can respect your brother-in-law's right to smoke, but you needn't allow him to smoke in your home.

When you encounter people whose values radically conflict with yours, you'll experience a hard truth: living your values can be challenging. When the conflict involves family members, friends, or close coworkers, the challenge will feel even tougher. That is why you must reflect long and hard before choosing and declaring your values.

If you wish your values to truly serve you, you must remain consciously aware of them every day. When you are not conscious of them, you open the door to your hardwired instincts—your shadow values, avoidance of discomfort and instant gratification. You'll discover once again that those instincts can quickly override your values and cause you to behave in unintended ways.

A Story of the Power of Instant Gratification

In early 2024, a prominent city government official in Los Angeles was convicted and sentenced to a thirteen-year prison term for bribery and corruption for his role in awarding huge construction contracts to major developers. In his letter seeking leniency (which was unsuccessful), he stated that many enticing gift offers had been dangled in front of him, and he had lacked the moral strength to act with integrity by rejecting them. Instead he chose instant gratification.

He now has ample time to reflect on his actions.

Step Two: Understanding How Your Values Work

Your values create their effects in tell-and-show scenarios. You create expectations by announcing your values (tell). You demonstrate their validity when your behavior aligns with your words (show). If you fail to deliver (or fail to show), significant consequences ensue, the costliest being the loss of others' trust.

Suppose, for instance, you see an ad on a website for a product that looks so appealing you feel that you must have it. You're hooked by the company's guarantee of 100 percent customer satisfaction. You order the product. It arrives. It doesn't work. You click onto the company's website to learn how to return the product and find that the company has a no-return policy. You call the customer service number and listen to the voice message telling you it doesn't accept calls. Would you ever trust that company again? What if every product you purchased on Amazon failed to perform? Would you continue to use Amazon?

As you proclaim your values, think of yourself as the product you want others to trust. If you don't live your values, why would anyone trust you? Remember, choosing your values is critical, and reflecting deeply before you choose is equally so.

Instruction Guide

Below are four questions that will guide you as you identify your values. Do *not* attempt to complete this assignment in one sitting—or even two or three. These questions are intended to help you reflect deeply. Many answers will not come easily, and most will not come quickly. You may need weeks, and in some cases months, to uncover information stored in the deepest storage locker of your memory.

Relax. With enough time and focused attention, the information you seek will emerge. When it does, write it down—always with pen and paper. Write in snippets. You may ultimately craft your answers in the same way you might complete a jigsaw puzzle. Take one piece at a time.

Question One: What Are Your Values Today?

Many of us have not thought about our values for some time. Naming and explaining them off the top of your head may be impossible. You may wonder if you even have values. Prior to reading the definition in this chapter, you might have been unsure as to what precisely constitutes a value, let alone what values you have been living by.

The fact is, every human being has values. Even terrorists, criminals, and politicians have them. We may have different interpretations of what they are, what they represent, and how, when, and why we practice them—or ignore them in favor of something else (most likely our shadow values). Sometimes values go by other names: beliefs about how to live, codes of conduct, religious teachings, moral guidelines. Still, these are values.

In and of themselves, values are neither good nor bad. Not every value is legal, moral, or ethical. Many of us believe that values are a universal moral code and that anyone whose behavior is immoral, unethical, or illegal has no values. That is untrue. Those people have values based on their desired way to live. I know people whose values are greed, money, and power. We all have witnessed companies whose only value is to increase shareholder wealth—by whatever means necessary (think Volkswagen and its air pollutions scandal in 2015). ISIS members have values, and if one wishes to belong to ISIS, one must live by the values of the group. The Mafia has values, one of which is loyalty, and being disloyal to Mafia leaders can get a member killed. A Mafioso's loyalty feels to me like a strictly enforced value.

EXERCISE

Write out your answers to the following prompts with pen and paper:

- Write down the names and meanings of your values.
- List the specific behavioral characteristics that you see as vital to demonstrating the ways you live your listed values.

This list is your starting point. It will come into play later.

Question Two: Where, How, and From Whom Did You Learn Your Values?

None of us are born with values, but we do learn them when we're very young, typically from our parents or other adult authority figures. They are usually framed within the context of how to behave. Sometimes they are delivered with tenderness, sometimes with an onerous "or else" attached.

Those early values typically serve as our moral code of conduct throughout our childhood. For some of us, not living them resulted in tangible consequences, such as being grounded, losing a weekly allowance, or being forbidden to play certain games or spend time with specific people.

As a teenager, you may have learned additional values from peers, coaches, troop leaders, someone older you emulated, or groups you belonged to like the Girl or Boy Scouts or Little League. Those sources typically wielded more influence on us than our parents did because we felt a primal need to be accepted by our chosen group. Our groups often become our tribe, and we all are wired to be tribal.

After high school, whether you attended college, joined the military, got married and started a family, or moved directly into the world of work, until the age of twenty-five (when the human brain reaches full emotional development), you may have adopted additional values from those around you—for example, a professor, commanding officer, spouse, boss.

EXERCISE

Write a list of the people who taught or instilled in you the values you currently hold. Note the time in your life when you acquired each of these values and the circumstances in which you adopted them.

Question Three: How Well Have Your Values Served or Not Served You?

At times people abandon their values and choose to behave in ways that run contrary to those values they have expressed. That happens when the instincts hardwired in our brains at birth—avoidance of discomfort and instant gratification—override our values. We then behave in ways that align with one or both of those instincts, our shadow values.

While your shadow values can help you avoid danger—their primary purpose 300,000 years ago—today they can stunt your growth by causing you to resist change and avoid exploring and embracing new opportunities. They can land you in a whole lot of trouble by pushing you to enjoy the pleasure of the moment while blinding you to harmful long-term consequences of your acts.

Examples abound. Think about drinking and driving, smoking, or continuing to give in to a craving for sweets after you learn that you are prediabetic.

EXERCISE

To find out how well your values have served you, write out your answers to the following prompts:

- Reflect on the frequency with which you consciously choose to override certain values and behave in ways that contradict those values.
- Ask yourself whether the values you believe you live by are, in fact, situational behaviors rather than unconditional values.
- Reflect on how and how often specific values have been instrumental in helping you achieve goals, handle challenging situations, or earn the trust of others. Write down these specific values, including the places, times, and moments when they helped you.

Question Four: What Values Will You Choose Going Forward?

You are free to choose your values at any stage of your life. You can add new values, drop one or two or more, or choose to retain all the values you already have.

Neuroscience findings confirm that we can do this at any time in our lives, but keep in mind, your shadow values will never disappear.[1] They are always lurking, waiting to jump in whenever you fail to maintain conscious awareness of and act in accordance with your chosen values. Those shadow values offer you the comfort of the familiar and will forever exert a compelling hold on you.

Conscious awareness of your values and your will to live those values are the only way to override your shadow values and resist their lure.

EXERCISE

Write down the answers to the questions below using a pen and paper:

- Do your values serve you today in ways that align with your vision and your greater purpose?
- Will your values support you going forward?
- Have your values helped you live at your full potential?
- What criteria will you use to select the values you wish to live? Those criteria inform your choice of whether to stay with your current values or adopt new values.
- Do your values reflect who you truly are, or have you adopted them because you believe they represent who others think you should be and do? Do you hold your values because you think they make a good impression on others?
- Is it easy for you to keep your values in your everyday consciousness?
- If it is not easy, ask and answer the question, "What would it take for me to maintain continuous, conscious awareness of my values?"

- Can you look in the mirror and tell yourself that you are living your values?
- When you face any kind of new situation, how often do you opt for one of your shadow values—instant gratification or avoidance of discomfort?

The Four Criteria for New Values

As you assess how your current values have served you up to now and what values you will choose to live by as you move forward, determine whether each of your potential values aligns with the criteria listed below. You may have additional criteria. If so, use those along with the following four.

Criteria One: Authenticity

Do your values reflect the true you? You must choose values that serve you and not some external influence or influences that you seek to please. Living authentically makes you trustworthy. Pretending to be someone you are not will cause stress—and stress, as you know, is bad for your physical and mental health and wellbeing.

Joey's Story

I knew Joey in the early '90s. He was most proud of his perfect family life. He told everyone he knew that he treasured his family above everything and everyone. His family included his wife and two children, and his and his wife's parents, grandparents, aunts, and uncles. Joey had a good job, regularly went to church, and attended or participated in all his children's activities. Every Sunday was family day—church services, group dinners, conversations, and love.

Joey had just one small problem. He was sleeping with three other women. He couldn't stop. He was addicted to sex. He never confessed to it, although he regularly went to church confession. He had kept his secret hidden for three years before one day his wife went out to lunch with friends, and there, sitting in a corner booth at the restaurant, sat Joey kissing one of his lovers.

The entire family was quickly enveloped by anger and grief. Joey earnestly worked to explain that his transgressions did not diminish his love for his wife. The other women, he said, provided him physical relief, a way to deal with his addiction. But his pleas fell on deaf ears. At the time, few had heard of sex addiction as a psychological condition. The family saw Joey as a dishonest, unfaithful, and detestable husband.

Joey and his wife divorced. His children paid the price, as children usually do.

Could one of Joey's professed values have made a difference? In a different scenario, Joey might have spoken to his wife about his addiction, asked or begged for her support, sought professional help, and delivered a less demonstrative performance to the outside world of his "goodness." In other words, Joey could have been authentic. We'll never know where that might have led, but addiction, secrecy, and Joey's need for instant gratification claimed many victims.

Criteria Two: Self-Respect

Do your values enhance your self-respect? Self-respect can wear two hats. Here, it serves as one of your criteria. It can also become one of your values.

A cousin of authenticity, self-respect has nuanced differences. Being authentic makes you real. Self-respect makes you confident. Respecting yourself enables you to face daunting challenges with courage and clarity. It also enables you to aim high and helps you dismiss self-limiting beliefs about what you can achieve.

Without self-respect, you will harbor a subtle hollowness inside you. It quietly saps your confidence so slowly that you do not feel it until one day you are struck by a lightning bolt of awareness and you see for the first time what others likely have seen for a long time.

Jim's Story

Several years ago, I played tennis weekly with one of my neighbors, Jim. We had private tennis courts in the townhome community where I lived.

Jim was tall and skilled, having played in the junior division at Wimbledon when he was seventeen years old.

Yet I regularly beat him, but not because I was a better player. Jim smoked three packs of cigarettes a day. He lacked stamina. Each time we played, as our match wore on, he ran out of gas, which led him to make too many unforced errors. In other words, Jim beat himself.

After a year of weekly play, we paused our play for two months. When we resumed, Jim looked different. His complexion had changed from yellowish to a rosy glow. He seemed more energetic. I asked him about it.

He said, "I quit smoking."

"That's it?" I asked.

"Yes."

"How did you do it? Some sort of program, patches, what?"

"Cold turkey," he said. "I just stopped."

I was curious. Few people abruptly quit a three-pack-a-day smoking habit cold turkey.

"What made you want to quit," I asked.

He told me he enjoyed smoking when he was in his early twenties, so he began to smoke more. He slowly became addicted, but he never saw it that way. Smoking was just a thing he did. He didn't notice the gradual adverse health effects. His job was demanding—long hours, lots of travel. It took its toll. One day he looked at himself in the mirror and he did not like what he saw. He was in his late thirties, but his face said late forties.

He reflected on his core beliefs, returning to lessons his parents had taught him when he was young. "Never be a victim," they said. "Always rise above—any problem, any person, any threat. You must always find your inner strength."

He told me that he had been indifferent to what was happening as a result of smoking until that day when he looked in the mirror, and he could not ignore the message his face reflected back at him.

"Okay," I said. "But cold turkey? How the hell did you do that?"

"Simple," he said. "I picked up a cigarette and held it next to my face. Then I looked into the mirror and asked myself out loud, 'Who is stronger, me or this damn cigarette?' And I never smoked again."

I asked him if a loss of self-respect contributed to his smoking. He paused to think and answered that he'd never thought of it that way, but yes. And diminished self-respect also reduced his self-confidence in other areas of his life. Self-respect was one of the basic rules his parents had taught him. For a long time, he said, he had lost that connection when it came to his smoking and its hold on him. He felt ashamed for ceasing to be the man his parents had taught him to be. He resolved to maintain his conscious awareness. He told me he was also changing his behavior in other areas of his life where his self-confidence had slipped.

It was an important conversation for us. Afterward, we sat quietly for a few minutes, until he smiled and said, "Let's play." And he proceeded to kick my butt. I confess, a small part of me wished for him to resume his smoking.

Reflecting on our conversation, I realized that Jim's cigarettes represented instant gratification, brought about by a lapse in his conscious awareness of a core value he chose to reconnect to—self-respect. He had been blinded from seeing his mental and physical health deteriorate, but when he performed a self-executed intervention, he regained his self-respect, overrode his shadow instinct, and put his life back on track.

Criteria Three: Measurability

Do your values enable you to self-assess how and how well you are living them? You must have control of the behaviors needed to live by your values. And your values should be sufficiently tangible to make assessing your performance measurable. For example, if you choose *world peace* as one of your values, attempting to assess your performance will prove to be too subjective. You might convince yourself you're living your values by saying, "Someone cut in front of me in the checkout line at the market, and I didn't shoot him, so I'm contributing to world peace." Did you really?

Let's suppose one of your values is integrity. To you, integrity means keeping your commitments and doing the right thing. You should be able to assess whether or not you are acting with integrity in every applicable situation, regardless of how others may act.

Oscar's Story

Years ago, a mutual friend introduced me to Oscar, a guy at the gym in Venice, California, where the three of us worked out. Oscar was a Vietnam veteran. He had served three consecutive combat tours in the infantry, totaling thirty-nine months, all spent fighting in the jungle.

Before he enlisted, Oscar had dropped out of high school, worked menial jobs, and lived to survive. Upon returning from Vietnam, Oscar had no job, no family, and no coping skills. Our government provided no support programs for veterans like Oscar. He was highly skilled in jungle survival and killing people, and he was emotionally, psychologically, and financially broke. He lived homeless and hopeless on the streets—mostly in a drunken haze—for five years.

Then, through a bizarre set of events that involved Oscar's arrest for assault and his ultimate release into the custody of the man he attacked (the friend who introduced us), Oscar began to turn his life around. He took courses and got his GED. He stopped drinking. He became religious.

During this journey, Oscar decided that giving back was his life's greater purpose. He started a transitional housing program for Vietnam veterans released from prison. The program was designed for veterans who lived in the house to help each other. No mental health professionals were involved. No counselors or social workers. And it worked. With grants, donors, and sponsors providing financial resources, Oscar's program grew to include multiple houses around the country and became one of the most successful transitional programs of its kind in the country, with the lowest recidivism rate ever recorded.

As he was growing this program, Oscar and I became friends. We worked out together in the morning, then walked to breakfast at a nearby popular haunt. On one of those mornings, I asked him to tell me how he had done all he had.

He described the steps, how he got his first sponsor, a real estate investor, to purchase the first house and how that led to introductions to more donors and other support. He talked about the house rules the people in the program had to obey and that those who did not were unceremoniously kicked out.

"But," I asked him one morning, "is there one thing that makes you appealing to your sponsors, one thing that makes you different?"

"Damn right there is," he said. "I have integrity. I keep my promises. When I commit, I deliver. Every time, with every person."

"With all the unknowns you have to deal with, that's a tall order," I said. "You're talking about guys you don't know and who don't know each other and are coming in right out of prison. A lot could go wrong."

Oscar gave me a blank stare, followed by a short, intense lecture.

"You corporate asses, you suits, you don't know squat about integrity and keeping commitments. Lemme tell you how integrity works on the street. Let's say you borrow ten dollars from me on Monday. I tell you I need my money back by Thursday. You promise me you'll get me my money back on time. If you don't keep your promise, you'll be dead before sunrise on Friday. Now that's integrity. That's how commitments work on the street. That's the code I live by. And that's what's helping build this program without any shrinks or government BS."

Oscar looked at me and calmed down. "Hey, I didn't mean nothin' personal when I talked about suits. I think you're a straight-up dude or I wouldn'a said that."

I thanked Oscar for what was probably the most profound graduate course lecture I'd ever heard on the meaning and measurability of integrity. Then we enjoyed some great blueberry pancakes.

But back to measurability and values that are not values. If, for example, you decide that *mutual respect* is one of your values, you will have created a problem. You can control your behavior, but you cannot control the behavior of people with whom you interact. Instead, choose *respect* as your value because you will have total control of living your value regardless of others' behavior.

If you accept conditional behavior for any of your values and for how you live them when you are challenged, depending on your frame of mind at the time, your behavior will be subjective. That opens the door for divided opinions between you and the rest of the world as to whether or not you live your values, and the result will be that others will trust you less and less.

You can effectively measure and assess your performance only when your rules of engagement (how you live your values) are thoroughly unconditional.

EXERCISE

Follow the prompts below, writing with pen and paper.

- Make a list of all the people you consider to be good friends. For example, let's say you have thirty people who are good friends for a variety of reasons—you have shared interests, you work together, your kids are friends with their kids, you're longtime neighbors, and so on.
- Deeply examine the quality of those thirty friendships using trust, vulnerability, and intimacy as your criteria. How many close friends do you actually have, and how many of those people do you have a nice relationship with? If you started with thirty friends, you will most likely determine that six or so of them are your true friends. The others are situational relationships.

Various behavioral studies over a number of years confirm that approximation. It's often referred to as the *80/20 rule*: 20 percent of your relationships generate 80 percent of the deep trust you receive from true friendships.

It works the same way with your values. Having a short list of a few unconditional values you commit to living will be far more valuable than will having a long list of good intentions that you mistakenly call values but wind up yielding inconsistent performance.

EXERCISE

Write out your answers to the following prompts:

- Make a list of values you believe you hold but that require reciprocal behavior from others.
- Ask yourself, "What would it take to make those values unconditional?"—if you chose to do so.
- Select those values that you can make unconditional and place these on your list of potential values going forward.
- Remove from consideration those that you choose not to make unconditional. They are now in the category of situationally desirable beliefs.

Criteria Four: Alignment with Your Vision and Greater Purpose

Do your values align with your vision and your greater purpose? When all the elements of your foundation are aligned with one another, you create clarity, focus, and seamless interaction. Potential conflict between your beliefs and your actions never occurs. Your problem-solving skills are at their peak, as is your mental energy and your enthusiasm. Your brain health is optimized because your brain is receiving optimal amounts of dopamine and serotonin.

Values that conflict with your vision or purpose will, at times, force you to make compromising choices. The resulting inner conflict produces stress. When under prolonged stress, your brain receives insufficient amounts of dopamine and serotonin, two chemicals essential for optimum brain health. Instead, your brain receives elevated levels of adrenaline and cortisol. Your memory and problem-solving skills diminish. Your progress and results will suffer. Prolonged stress can cause a rise in blood pressure, which can increase your risk of suffering a heart attack.

Let's say your vision involves a community-building activity that will enrich the lives of the people living in a low-income section of your city. You must build a strong team, delegate authority, and address challenges collaboratively to realize your vision. One of your values is self-reliance. You have always solved problems alone, and you don't delegate well. But following your vision demands that you build strong teams and allow others to come up with solutions.

You have now created a self-inflicted inner conflict. You must choose between self-reliance and pursuing your vision.

Conflicts of that nature sometimes yield unexpected benefits. In the example above, the situation invites the question, "What would it take for you to abandon your value of self-reliance and instead adopt a value of collaboration, teamwork, or adaptability?" A time for reflection, perhaps.

The Two Types of Values

There are two types of values for you to consider:

- Moral values
- Goal-oriented values

When humans created values, they were embraced as prevailing moral standards. In today's world, we can have values that support our vision, our goals, and our greater purpose. The two varieties can easily work together to help you live and achieve at your full potential.

For example, you might choose *living a healthy lifestyle* as one of your values. That will likely require you to embrace learning continuously, eating better, exercising, doing yoga, and meditating—all combined so as to improve the health and longevity of both your brain and your body. That value will improve your effectiveness as you move toward your vision.

Three Values for You to Consider

Here are three achievement-oriented values for your consideration. Each one relates to navigating your course in a rapidly changing world:

- *Adaptability*—The value of adaptability means you purposefully seek, welcome, and embrace new ideas, new courses of action, and new relationships—especially those that challenge your instinctive desire to avoid leaving your comfort zone. Being adaptive helps you gain new knowledge and learn new skills that expose you to new opportunities.
- *Listening*—The value of listening means you aim to truly hear and understand what others mean when they speak or write. You commit to hear the sights and sounds of your environment when they speak to you as you walk—on a beach, in the hills, in a crowded shopping mall, or on a city street. You also allow the entire message to penetrate your consciousness before you judge the motive, message, or messenger. You hear both what is being said and what is not being said.
- *Empathy*—Building on listening, you express empathy when you listen to others to fully understand their message and their feelings about the message from their perspective without judging them. Empathy is a learned skill, improved through practice and feedback. It contradicts our hardwired instinct to judge.

Each of us possesses a unique sense of reality, constructed from a compilation of perceptions and interpretations of the meanings of all the events in our lives and further shaped by conscious and unconscious biases. In the context of our human experience, pure objectivity is impossible. That fact underscores the need for us to learn to listen and to hear others' realities if we seek to build bonds of understanding.

But the overriding reason to seek to become empathetic is this: your ability to express empathy is the most powerful skill you will ever possess to help you build trust. And that's a fact.

EXERCISE

From everything you have absorbed in this chapter, combined with your already existing values, complete the steps below in writing:

- Create the list of your values.
- Define them in writing.
- Explain the ways in which you will demonstrate living them.

Study your list. Make certain that

- Your choices are unconditional.
- You are committed to living them.
- You can assess your performance.
- They align with your vision (and your greater purpose, when you define it).

Living these values will move you forward with clarity and purpose in your next chapter. Be sure the number of values you have chosen is manageable. More than ten is likely to prove unwieldy.

Now breathe, relax, and prepare to address our next question: why are you here?

CHAPTER SEVEN

GREATER PURPOSE

The heart of human excellence often begins to beat when you discover a pursuit that absorbs you, frees you, challenges you, or gives you a sense of meaning, joy, or passion.

—TERRY ORLICK

When Henry David Thoreau wrote, "The mass of men lead lives of quiet desperation," I believe he was describing any person whose life has no *why*.

How much thought have you given to asking yourself why were you born? We were all born with a why. That why is the foundation of our greater purpose. It is our purpose beyond survival. Our why can point us to do what in some way, large or small, will make a difference in the world.

We are meant to bring our greater purpose to life and share it with those we directly and indirectly touch. Some of us become aware of our greater purpose early in life before we've had a host of experiences to shape our basis for discovering it.

For others, experiences over time provide signs that help us discover our greater purpose. That process of discovery describes my journey—learning, unlearning, molding, interpreting, shaping, becoming aware, and living through periods of spiritual numbness and self-centeredness, focused only on comfortable survival. All that, combined with deep reflection, revealed a clear sense of my greater purpose—to help enrich lives through writing.

In chapter 5 you read about three people whose visions were grand and intended to be world-changing:

- Mother Teresa, whose vision was to care for the poorest of the poor
- Elie Wiesel, whose vision led him to help us remember the horrors of the Holocaust so we never repeat them
- Dr. Martin Luther King Jr., whose vision was of genuine equality for all people

Those three people seamlessly aligned and entwined their respective visions and their greater purpose. As a result, they were always simultaneously striving toward both.

Each of those visions and lives of greater purpose shared a common thread, one that contains three ingredients. These three ingredients provided Mother Teresa, Wiesel, and King with the emotional fuel and passion they needed to make purpose come alive.

Any greater purpose, of any size or scope, should be guided by these three ingredients:

- *Personal*—Your greater purpose must reflect the true you, your authenticity, your honest motives, and your motivations.
- *Powerful*—Your greater purpose must embody you fully engaged and acting with passion at your full potential.
- *Possible*—Your greater purpose must be actionable. You are able to do—not just think or imagine or wish but do what is needed to make your purpose meaningful and relevant in the ways it touches others.

You have the power to control those ingredients. Mother Teresa, Wiesel, and King had visions that focused on caring, remembering, and moral equality. But even the noblest ideas have no energy of their own until someone with the right vision and purpose breathes life into them. The same is true of any greater purpose, including yours.

Whether your greater purpose impacts the lives of two people or two hundred or two billion, its core principle remains the same. It involves you doing what you were put on this earth to do.

Far too many of us have never questioned why we are here. Are we too focused on the day-to-day menus of our lives? Are we afraid to look? Or have we simply never thought about this notion? What would it take to stop and step back far enough to see the way our greater purpose can play out within the context of our lives?

Some of us might believe, as did our ancient ancestors, that our only purpose is to survive and procreate. Unlike our ancestors' options, today's world offers us a large palette of choices as to the level of comfortable survival we can achieve. If your perceived purpose is based purely on material achievements, it remains a purpose framed within the context of survival. While living that way is certainly not a crime (I lived that way for sixty years), it does circumscribe you to live a life devoid of opportunities to find your greater purpose and the fulfillment awaiting you when you discover and pursue it.

Many of us might believe that we are too small and too insignificant, that we can't possibly have anything to offer the world that can actually make a difference. In that framework of thought, purpose is your only reality, and greater purpose resides in the realm of others. But the fact is, you are not too small, you are not too insignificant, you do have something to offer the world that will make a difference.

As the Dalai Lama said, "Anyone who thinks that they are too small to make a difference has never tried to fall asleep with a mosquito in the room."

When I read that I laughed and instantly remembered my experience nearly thirty years ago while on an African safari. The safari literature informed everyone in our group that a mosquito bite could cause malaria. Our guides told us that only the mosquitos that came out at night carried malaria. Those, they told us, were the dangerous ones. One night, as I lay in bed in my hotel room on the Serengeti Plain in Tanzania, tired and falling asleep, I heard a faint buzz. I turned on the light and saw the little critter—a mosquito. Instantly I was wide awake. Game on. I pursued him, rolled up magazine in hand. I struck. He zigged and zagged. I missed. Two hours of lost sleep chasing him until I finally nailed the little sucker. Exhausted and victorious, I quickly fell asleep.

Today, I marvel at how, as I sit here in the year 2024, twenty-seven years after the event, my memory of that little mosquito buzzing around my hotel room, minding his own business, threatening my well-being with his presence, hurls me back in time as if my safari experience happened yesterday. The Dalai Lama knew what he was talking about, and his message is clear.

No one is too small to make a difference—somehow, somewhere, to someone. So it is with you and your greater purpose.

Each of us has a unique gift. That gift is what makes you, you. Many of us don't realize that fact or know what our gift is. Some may know they have a gift but may not recognize its uniqueness. They believe that many people have that same gift, and this means that they and their gift are not special. If you believe that, *stop it*. You are wrong.

For fifty years, I believed that everyone knew what I knew, that nothing about me or what I knew was special. I was wrong.

My wife, Arlene, had that same belief. She too was wrong.

Arlene's Story of Her Unique Gift

Arlene has a special gift. She was born with a condition known as *synesthesia*. It is rare but not mysterious. It occurs at birth. When all babies are born, all their sensory neurons—those that control sight, smell, taste, touch, and hearing—are packed together in a single ball. Immediately upon birth, the neurons are sent to their designated locations within our brains. Thus we see with our eyes, hear with our ears, taste with our tongues, and so on.

Sometimes, however, a few neurons fail to get the memo and travel to the wrong area of the brain. In Arlene's case, some of her taste neurons wound up in the area of her brain that controls sight.

As a result, Arlene can taste with her eyes. She can look at almost any item of food that she is seeing for the first time and can describe its taste. Her gift is eerie and amazing.

Arlene lived much of her life believing that everyone could do this. It took me five years, beginning from the time we married, to convince her that no one else I know can taste with their eyes. At long last she recognized her unique gift.

Now Arlene uses her synesthesia, combined with years of intensive nutrition research, to take food that contains unhealthy ingredients and change those unhealthy ingredients to healthy ones to produce delicious, far healthier variations. For example, Arlene makes brownies from zucchini, and they are as delicious as any brownies I have ever eaten. They're also healthier. No one who tastes them ever knows they're made from zucchinis.

Once Arlene acknowledged her gift, she decided to use it to help others willing to listen to eat healthier, thus to feel better and to improve their state of wellness. She intensively studies nutrition with the goal of developing recipes that have been scientifically shown to enhance brain health and wellness and to ease chronic conditions caused by inflammation. Today, her biggest challenge is convincing people to give up their tasty but toxic eating habits in favor of adopting healthier eating regimens—regimens that are equally tasty. By discovering and applying her unique gift, Arlene has moved from passive interest to focused passion. And I'm her lucky test pilot, so I taste how truly gifted she is. Still, whenever we walk past a bakery and Arlene looks in the window and describes how the various breads and pastries taste, I freak out.

Like Arlene, by recognizing and harnessing your gift and using it with passion, whatever your gift is, you can help others. That help can be dramatic, or it can be subtle.

Eddie's Story

In 2002, I encountered a particular TSA agent at Cleveland Hopkins International Airport. It's widely known that being a TSA agent is a thankless job. It doesn't pay well, and agents put up with a lot of abuse heaped on them by disgruntled travelers, some of whom blame their TSA agent for everything that is wrong with travel and our country.

Eddie was a TSA agent at Hopkins. But Eddie was different. He put on a show for groups of travelers moving through his line. He animatedly talked about and demonstrated the importance of safety—how belt buckles could become lethal weapons, toxic chemicals could be hidden inside shoes, or explosive devices could be packed into children's strollers. And Eddie turned all that knowledge and experience into a comedic theatrical performance delivered throughout his entire shift. Many travelers applauded. People chose Eddie's line, even when on both sides of him other agents had shorter lines. Airport personnel advised travelers that they could get through faster if they moved to another line, but people refused. "I want to stay in this line. I want to hear him," they'd say, pointing at Eddie.

As I made my way through the line, I caught Eddie's attention. "You're amazing," I told him. "How the hell did you come up with this?"

"Listen, man," he said. "Everyone knows what I do is a rotten job. It don't pay much. But it's the job I got. I told myself, as long as I got to do this, I might as well make everybody's life as good as I can make it. I do it for them. I also do it for me. I actually got to likin' gettin' up in the mornin.'"

Eddie had a gift. Eddie knew it. Eddie used it.

I guessed Eddie to be in his fifties. I asked him what he planned to do later in life. He told me he didn't know for sure, but whatever it was, it had to be around making people feel better about themselves.

I remember thinking as I walked through the terminal after my encounter with Eddie that he has a purpose in life: to make people feel better about themselves, as only Eddie could. He succeeded with me.

Stan's Story

Some people's paths can be described as a life in search of a purpose. But those who discover and pursue their greater purpose when they are young usually follow the path of their purpose in search of a life.

Stan's life falls into the latter category. He is blessed and cursed with a hyperactive, curious, highly intelligent conceptual mind. Blessed in the sense that he has extraordinary abilities to see what most people cannot. But cursed in the sense that since most people cannot see or conceptualize as Stan can, too often others don't understand what the hell he is talking about.

That poses a great challenge for Stan because his greater purpose is to teach, though not in a conventional classroom setting. He earned his doctorate in mathematics and, in his twenties and thirties, he taught calculus at several universities and colleges, including the

University of Michigan, Mount Holyoke, and Smith College. While that experience aligned with his greater purpose, teaching in a school setting proved too confining. It did not offer his intellect and curiosity the range of exploration for which they hungered.

Stan began to plant the seeds for discovering his greater purpose when, at the age of six, he decided he was agnostic. How does a six-year-old determine that God is superfluous in the grand scheme of how the universe works? Stan did—at least enough to support his personal beliefs. He attempted to enlighten his Orthodox Jewish grandfather of this truth, but Stan's logic did not go over well. This was his first brush with trying to teach an unhearing audience. After that, and before he was ten, he became interested in philosophy, mathematics, and science. Playing in Little League never appeared on his radar screen of desired childhood pursuits.

After Stan left his institutional teaching life, he shifted his focus to consulting and advising companies and their leaders in a variety of business entities and government agencies. While working to solve complex business challenges, he always injected a healthy dose of philosophy about the inherent goodness of people and the need for everyone to work toward creating a more just and fairer world. He was teaching. People always respected Stan, but they did not always hear or act on his message. In fact, people seldom heeded Stan, but that never deterred him. Greater purpose cannot be defeated in the court of public opinion.

About twenty-five years ago, Stan's visionary eyes saw an emerging threat that few acknowledged. As a result, Stan found what turned out to be his niche, the path on which he is able to ardently pursue his greater purpose.

What Stan saw was the threat posed by cybercrime and the need for people to protect themselves against cybercriminals. Cybersecurity called out to him. Everyone, he knew, must be made cybersafe. Lives and livelihoods depended on it.

In a variety of roles and within several different structures, cybersecurity has since been Stan's dogged pursuit. Learning and mastering detection protocols to prevent crimes and responding to mitigate damages when attacks occur, protecting people and property from what is now widely acknowledged as a cybercrime pandemic—that is Stan's mission. Today he is the founder and CEO of a cybersafety organization. In late 2023 he celebrated his eightieth birthday. If you ask him about pursuing his greater purpose, he will tell you that he is just getting started.

Stan's path is a lesson for people who feel the calling of their greater purpose at a young age. The path is seldom smooth and easy. Just because you know your purpose, you are not guaranteed that everyone will line up to support you. Your clarity of purpose must withstand rejection by people who disagree with or don't truly understand what you are about. You must stay the course—as Stan is doing.

The Story of Many Other Artists

Many artists, writers, dancers, and actors fall into the category of people who find their greater purpose when they are young. In their own ways, they are all storytellers, and they each create a distinctly different impression in the minds and hearts of people who experience their work. No two are alike. But these individuals often lift us out of our doldrums, aid us in our struggles, entertain us, engage us, relieve us, and inspire us. Passion and purpose usually grab them by the heart and soul and will not let go. And their life's path becomes unshakeable.

Years ago in my consulting practice, I witnessed an illustration of this kind of passion and purpose. One of my clients was a major motion picture studio, and I was working with an administrative division whose work required ensuring that the studio received its proper share of royalties from all its intellectual properties.

Thirty-five people worked in that department. Their work was clerical and tedious, not creative in any sense. Oddly, every person working in that department was an aspiring screenwriter. They ranged in age from twenty-five to sixty. Every one of them was striving to write a screenplay that would be green-lighted and made into a hit movie. All of them realized at a young age that their greater purpose in life revolved around writing. They all intended to write until they died. They all spent their time away from their day job writing. Their conversations during work breaks and lunch hours revolved around their writing.

All these individuals worked at the studio to pay their bills and breathe the same air and rub elbows with other creative people. All of them shared the same dream and approached writing in their own unique way. No two were alike. Despite years of rejections, their passion and faith remained unshakeable. They were intense but not obsessed. They focused on their work at the studio with professional dedication. They excelled at their jobs. Yet their passion for writing was palpable. I found them interesting, engaging, and inspiring to be around, although I had not yet established my love affair with writing.

The Importance of Purpose

Given that so many people are either not aware of or not committed to pursuing their greater purpose, you may wonder why greater purpose is so important. Couldn't we do just as well without having one? What's wrong, you may be asking, with being focused on what's on our plate without concerning ourselves with this aspirational stuff?

To answer those questions, to understand the value of and need for a greater purpose, we must begin at the beginning. How did greater purpose become relevant?

As you'll recall from earlier chapters, 300,000 years ago our purpose was to survive and, if we made it into adulthood, to procreate.

Today, we all are born with that same fundamental purpose—to survive. Survival is universal, regardless of our circumstances. From those who are penniless to those who are prosperous, we all share this common purpose.

You do, however, have opportunities to make numerous choices that give meaning and depth to your life beyond survival. Your purpose can expand from seeking individual comfort and success to include building and nurturing a family. And it can extend beyond family in numerous ways. You might choose philanthropy—for instance, volunteering time to serve a worthwhile cause, starting a foundation, engaging in social activism for something you believe in, becoming involved in city government, rescuing dogs or cats, saving the environment. Most people live their lives within those sorts of context of purpose.

And these chosen activities and engagements may relate to your desired legacy, your greater purpose. If so, fine.

But if you are doing any of this kind of work purely out of a sense of duty or because you believe others will respect you for doing it or because it is a family tradition you don't care to break, you are likely experiencing satisfaction but not gratification. You are happy, but not quite fulfilled.

If that describes you, know that greater opportunity beyond mere satisfaction awaits you. Identifying and pursuing your greater purpose is that opportunity.

The notion of having a unique gift may sound blue-sky aspirational to some of you. You may believe that unique gifts exist only on a global scale. You may recognize a gift when you experience it coming from a superstar entertainer, a brilliant scientist who develops a cure for a previously incurable disease, or an inventor who creates something no one knew they needed but once introduced becomes a thing no one can live without, such as the iPhone.

And yes, it is possible to live well beyond survival, do good things, give back, and help people, neighborhoods, cities, and society as a whole, all without connecting to your greater purpose. You may choose to write checks to charities, special interest groups, and political causes, and you may do so without truly engaging. Obviously, you are doing good, perhaps a great deal of good, but if you are not personally involved and emotionally invested in some way that adds unique value because of your presence, you are not pursuing your greater purpose.

For many of us (I suspect the majority of people), our awareness of our special gift has a long incubation period. The primary reason for this is that if we do not become aware of our special gift when we are young, we usually don't frame our lives within the context of pursuing our greater purpose. Instead, we conceive and achieve goals along the spectrum of survival.

We need to have many life experiences to bring our gift into focus, and usually that focus requires much reflection about how what we know and do is unique in how it resonates and creates an impact others cannot replicate.

Take me, for example. My deep attachment to writing began when I was sixty years old. In the beginning, writing was my hobby but not my greater purpose. As I continued to write, my feelings intensified. Over the next fifteen years, my relationship with writing methodically progressed from my being interested to my being engaged to my being passionate. Before that awakening at sixty, I was heavily involved in my consulting career. I remained focused on comfortable survival. I was good at my work and so preoccupied with it, I could not see beyond it.

By the time I was sixty, I discovered that my gift as a consultant was my ability to metaphorically connect the dots of seemingly unrelated events in ways most others did not see. I used those connections to unearth new opportunities for growth. And as I took writing classes, comments made by a couple of my writing instructors provided a clue as to my gift. My instructors told me that the strength of my writing lay in my willingness to tell the unvarnished truth. My writing, they said, was adequate. My truth-telling was appealing and unique.

Over the next fifteen years, I had many conversations with a variety of people, both in and outside the world of business. From those conversations I gleaned the idea that I could use my ability to connect disparate dots in my writing, which might become my path to reaching many more people, to helping others far beyond my clients discover and utilize their unique gifts. And thus I could find fulfillment in ways that I could not achieve in my business pursuits.

I found my greater purpose. It took just seventy-five years.

"Why did it take that long?" I asked myself.

I needed reflection to provide the answers to that question. I began by focusing on my vision. To my shock I realized for the first sixty years of my life, I had none. I spent years in my business facilitating and coaching company leaders to create their organization's vision, and somehow, I never considered creating my own.

My logic was clear, understandable, and dysfunctional. As I have described in earlier chapters, as a young child I was taught that comfortable survival should be my goal in life. I saw no reason to look beyond that. I was financially comfortable. I had found intellectual satisfaction in my work. I told myself that was enough.

Those first sixty years coincided with the years I spent unwilling to be vulnerable. Reflecting more deeply helped me see that by not allowing myself to be vulnerable in my personal relationships, I was also suppressing my feelings in other areas of life. I equated intellectual satisfaction with passion and comfortable survival with purpose. At that time, I saw no need for anything more. I allowed my thoughts to suppress my feelings. Another blind spot.

In my experience, many people have a vision, and everyone, though they may not be aware, has values. But most of us overlook our greater purpose. It is the most challenging of the three ingredients we need to sense and feel and grow. And because it is the most challenging, it is also the easiest to ignore.

So many of us spend our lives busily addressing our many thoughts and events and activities and goals and accumulating enough stuff (money and the satisfying but not necessarily fulfilling things it can buy). Greater purpose, if you sense the need for it at all, often surfaces when your life takes a turn and you begin walking a new path. Suddenly there it is, appearing out of nowhere, standing in the middle of the road, demanding that you give it a good hard look.

When that happens, and you look at it, you might think "Why haven't I seen this before?" As you reflect, you come to realize how your skills, experiences, and desire to make a difference have coalesced to produce this magic moment of awareness. And you begin to act on it.

Some of you have not yet accepted the fact that you have a unique gift, so you don't yet believe that when you deliver your gift as only you can, you will make a difference, and the world will be better for it. And because you aren't delivering it, you are robbing yourself of the feeling of fulfillment that awaits you. It is a reality that, for you, does not exist—yet.

Some of you will have recognized your greater purpose for some time, but life has gotten in the way. You have not as yet been able to find a way to pursue it. Many of you believe you do have a greater purpose but don't yet know what it is, and until you do, you cannot bring it to life. And the sad fact is this: too many people live their entire lives without ever discovering their greater purpose.

Transitioning from your present life to a new chapter, one in which your future is not a continuation of your past, presents an ideal window of opportunity to reflect, enabling you to see your gift and understand your passions, especially those you have felt but not explored. You must be discerning in this process.

And you must ask yourself, "Are these passions or are these mere fantasies?"

My Story: Fantasy

As a teenager I dreamed of pursuing a career as a tennis player. The fact that I began playing ten years later than I should have and that I did not have the elite athletic skills needed to play at a world-class level didn't stop me from dreaming. It also didn't stop me from playing and practicing as if I could pursue that dream. When I reflect on those years, I realize that my obsession with tennis was my way of escaping from loneliness and feelings of being not enough that plagued me during that stage of my development. Tennis was a great crutch for me, a bridge to early adulthood. And I did get good enough to thoroughly enjoy the game. I even got to rub elbows and hit with some players who pursued professional careers. Once I started college, I no longer fantasized about tennis. I focused on getting an education that could lead to landing a job that would enable me to comfortably survive. Another rabbit hole.

My Story: Passion

Elements of my greater purpose began to slowly seep into my consciousness after I left the field of public accounting when I was twenty-six. As a CPA working for an outstanding firm and dealing with a diverse group of clients, I became less interested in the analytical world of numbers and more attracted to the human side of business. I was offered and accepted a management position with one of my firm's clients, a privately owned company. Mentally and emotionally, I was still operating in comfortable survival mode, but I had identified and acted on my need to find greater fulfillment in a new area of business.

Although I did not consciously see it, that was the beginning of my search for my greater purpose. Of course, I had much to experience and volumes to learn. I needed to identify, articulate, and consciously live my values and recognize that a few of my values, acquired during early childhood, did not serve me well. Survival, self-reliance, and never being vulnerable were strangling my growth, but I didn't realize that for years. My survival focus blocked me from imagining a personal vision—or even considering the idea of one. It also blocked me from imagining a greater purpose. Having a satisfying, well-paying job defined the limits of my imagination, and my need to be seen as excelling kept me from pursuing challenging opportunities that would have taken me too far out of my comfort zone.

One offer I received during my career, though, stands out in my memory. When I was in my early forties, I was offered a position as the head of ancillary product development at a relatively new company, Lucasfilm (producers of *Star Wars*, *Indiana Jones*, and others). I would be reporting to George Lucas. The position was out of my comfort zone. I turned it down. In retrospect, that episode was a stunning illustration of how my self-limiting beliefs prevented me from growing in ways that would expand my creative horizons. In the presence of filmmakers and screenwriters, I might have been able, years earlier, to see and pursue my interest in writing. That job might have helped me identify my greater purpose years earlier than I did. We'll never know.

Still, with all my self-imposed limits, I increased my knowledge and improved my skills, and I advanced my career but never beyond my self-limiting beliefs as to what I could do. As I progressed, however, I did begin to sense the possibility that I had a unique skill. I came to see that not everyone could piece together seemingly disparate events, metaphorically connect behavioral dots and conceive innovative strategies the way I could. I applied that skill in a number of situations with many companies before I accepted that I had a unique ability that was, perhaps, my gift.

Accepting my gift unlocked my desire to explore growth possibilities, in both my work and my personal life. My acceptance contributed to my willingness to examine my resistance to being vulnerable. And that led me to enroll in the workshop in Hawaii that I wrote about in chapter 1.

In essence, I devoted fifteen years, from the age of sixty to seventy-five, to reflecting, reexamining, reframing, and changing my early life perspectives about what constituted my truths, establishing more constructive realities, casting aside values that did not serve me, and choosing new ones that did.

During that period, I found myself, and I liked what I found. I came to believe in myself, embrace vulnerability, and see it as a strength, not a weakness. I met, fell in love with, and married the woman of my dreams and accepted the fact that I was the man of hers (or at least a reasonable facsimile). And in this new skin, I was free to envision my future, our future, one not inextricably bound to the past.

I was able to imagine using my recently discovered passion for writing to fulfill my greater purpose, one dedicated to helping people in many walks of life build their own foundations, forge their own destinies, and discover, pursue, and live in the land of their greater purpose.

So why did it take me seventy-five years to find my greater purpose? Through reflection, I discovered that a combination of factors were involved:

- I spent almost sixty years rigidly focused on comfortable survival, achieving success within the boundaries of my self-limiting beliefs (perhaps my only regret in life).
- I attended personal development workshops over a nine-year period. These workshops helped lead me to reflections that unearthed my child's mind—a mind that had implanted

in my unconscious brain a lot of dysfunctional beliefs and perceptions.
- I was able to rewrite my narrative about who I am and what I can achieve.
- I unlearned old dysfunctional perceptions and beliefs.
- Through the process of neuroplasticity, with rigorous repetitious practice, I was able to adopt new beliefs and skills.
- Putting my new beliefs and skills to use, I came to understand what it would take to guide me to where I want to go.

Can you guess which one item required, by far, the greatest amount of time?

Unlearning old beliefs and perceptions required 80 percent of those fifteen years. In essence, I spent twelve years unlearning to experience the benefits of three years of learning.

I tell you this so you understand that our unconscious minds wield that kind of power to form our beliefs. Many of our beliefs are self-limiting; they make our decisions and direct our lives. And far too many of us live our entire lives never consciously aware of any of that.

Your Next Steps

The process of identifying your unique gift and finding your greater purpose will help you more quickly gain focus, clarity, and direction. The context in which your greater purpose may come into play will help guide you when you are considering or have already chosen a path for your next chapter. Conscious awareness is all you need to recognize your greater purpose and allow it to enhance every aspect of your life

Following is a list of a few situations to help you consider how your greater purpose fits into the overall context of your next steps:

- *Change of pace*—Perhaps leading life at a slower pace will open doors, allowing you more time to reflect and thus to find enlightenment.
- *Change of place*—Moving to a different home, neighborhood, city, or even a different country often leads to exposing you to previously unimagined, exciting opportunities.
- *Change of lifestyle*—Adapting to the changes you'll experience by moving from a large city to a small town might enable you to live with less stress, have more time to engage in your hobbies, make new friends, and appreciate just being.
- *Financial needs that are different from your present level*—Experience more gratification with a less-is-more lifestyle. Don't feel the pressure to impress others by acquiring more stuff, or experience the inner peace you feel when you can be defined by who you are, not by what you have.
- *New relationships*—Embrace the reality that most of your situational friendships based on the common interests of your prior career will evaporate, and you will have the need and opportunity to find and form new relationships with an entirely new audience. This can open up unforeseen growth opportunities. Can you feel the quiet excitement?
- *Learning new skills, maybe a career change*—You will have the opportunity to recapture the child in you—a sponge with endless curiosity, an open mind, and a voracious appetite for learning. Your creativity will blossom. You will grow as a person.
- *Extensive travel*—Untethered at last, you will be free to see the places, do the things, and enjoy the experiences that you could never make time for during your working years. Charting your path with travel as a committed part of your journey can be exhilarating—if you allow it to be.
- *Change of family relationships in time and intensity*—You have the opportunity to spend more time (or perhaps less) with

cherished family members, yet you don't want to run the risk of overstaying your welcome. Collaborating with family members to achieve that perfect balance can open this next chapter to pure joy. And with that balance, you will position yourself to pursue other opportunities with greater peace of mind.

- *Health*—You may not have the physical strength and skills that you once enjoyed. Now you have the need and the opportunity to find balance in your next chapter. For example, you might pursue opportunities to coach rather than play. You might replace running with healthful walking.
- *Your passions for certain activities or pursuits*—Passions that you have not pursued because life's immediate needs got in the way are still available. If you have a passion that you love but abandoned because your lifestyle got in the way, you are now free to revisit that passion because competing priorities no longer exist. What would it take to pursue that passion and make it an integral part of your life?
- *Desire to give back*—You may have been philanthropic up to now but in ways that did not call for your personal presence. Perhaps you were financially but not emotionally invested. Perhaps you now have the opportunity to contribute your physical and emotional self to something you deem worthy, something where you can use your gift to make a difference in ways you and your recipients have not yet experienced.

EXERCISE

Answer the following prompts in writing with pen and ink on paper.

- Define your unique gift—if you essentially know what it is.

- Explain how you deliver that gift in your own way and to whom you deliver it.
- Imagine and write about the ways in which you might be able to make your gift centrally involved in the next chapter of your life.
- If you do not yet know what you believe to be your special gift, reflect and take the following steps:
    - Think back to situations and experiences at any time in your life when you contributed something special that touched people in unique ways.
    - Look for patterns over the years in which you delivered that same kind of uniqueness to other situations and how they affected people and outcomes.
    - Reflect on how you felt after those experiences. Joy? A sense of fulfillment? If not those, then what did you feel?
    - What are you passionate about? How do you or can you express those passions in ways that relate to other people?

Take a Moment

If you've reflected until your mind is drained, you don't have an ounce of reflection left to explore, and you have not yet discovered your greater purpose, know this. Your greater purpose is in you. It is buried but not dead. It lies in a place you have not yet discovered. Give yourself a break. Take time away. Do other things. Explore, embrace, and adopt other elements of your foundation—your vision and your values—that will help you enrich your next chapter. Somewhere in time, spontaneously, you will sense an opportunity to reflect. Seize it. Eventually the breakthrough moment will happen for you, as it does for all of us.

It took me seventy-five years. And it arrived, unannounced in words, but rich and clear in my experience. Stay the course.

Why Greater Purpose Is So Vitally Important

Choosing to not pursue your greater purpose is not a crime.

It is a shame.

Your greater purpose is not holy.

It is wholesome.

Living your greater purpose is not fancy.

It is fulfilling.

Fulfillment is a unique kind of spiritual magic that you can never experience by being merely satisfied.

In this next chapter of your life, why in the world would you deprive yourself of the joy of fulfillment?

Find it. Go for it.

CHAPTER EIGHT

PUTTING IT ALL TOGETHER

The map is not the territory.

—Alfred Korzybski

Your map consists of content: your vision, your values, and your greater purpose. Content is information. It is passive. It describes the territory you will navigate as you build your foundation. Content is not experience. Real-life actions you take and the results you experience in the process of building and using your foundation make up your territory.

To illustrate, picture this. You have read the definition and descriptions of the nature of values. You understand the importance of writing your values and their definitions and committing to living them. You are aware of how pervasive your values are in shaping your behavior. That information is your map.

You have an understanding, but you have not yet acted. Armed with your map, you set about naming and defining your values. You have now entered your territory.

As you write and reflect, you realize that some of your values no longer serve your needs. You adapt. You choose some new values you plan to adopt and existing values you decide to discard. And so it goes. All your real-life experiences happen in your territory.

You needed your map to get started, and from time to time, you will refer to it to guide you on your journey. But only your experience in your territory will create results.

I presented the three elements—vision, values, and greater purpose—in a particular sequence. You may think you should create your personal foundation following this same sequence. Not necessarily. Our minds often don't perform according to linear logic. Instead, our emotions trigger our actions, and feelings seldom follow an intellectually prescribed pattern.

Below I clarify the way your journey will play out and shape the ways in which you may build your foundation.

But first, you must know this:

- The process of creating and aligning your vision, values, and greater purpose is not an all-or-nothing effort. Do not think for a moment that unless you undertake all three, none will be effective. You will experience a measure of success with each element individually. If, for example, you choose to develop and live your values but elect not to pursue your vision and greater purpose at this time, you will still experience great benefit.
- You can develop each element in any order. Listen to and follow your inner voice. It will tell you what you need to address first.
- You need not complete one element before you work on another. Should you, for instance, first choose to develop your greater purpose because it is uppermost in your mind or because you have already begun searching for it, that's fine. While focused on your greater purpose, you may recognize that some of your values are not serving you well. If that

happens, shift your focus to your values. That is an effective way to achieve alignment between the elements. Alignment is essential to make all the elements work together seamlessly.

- With each step you take, you will experience incremental growth. For example, let's say you are exploring how to define your vision. Having identified six areas you want to explore, extensive travel is one of the six. Travel would be a new experience for you. As you investigate further, you begin to develop a greater awareness of the world around you. You become aware of places, people, customs, and cultures in other parts of the world that have always existed, but because you were not paying attention, they never existed for you. As you continue to delve into the other five areas you wish to explore, you will find that you are exploring each with a deeper level of curiosity.

With those four pieces of knowledge in hand, let's look at how you can apply them to create a foundation designed just for you.

The three elements of your foundation—vision, values, and greater purpose—are organic. This means each one automatically interacts with the other two. Information doesn't flow from one element to the next. Instead, your brain creates a connection loop between all three. That connection becomes the conduit for instinctive communication among and between all three elements.

Your emotions, not linear logic, drive this stream of unconscious communication. At any given moment you might be working on your vision, when suddenly, and for no apparent reason, your values begin to occupy your thoughts. That shift of focus originated in your unconscious mind, probably because your unconscious mind sensed that your values and vision were not aligned. Your unconscious mind informed your conscious mind, which then caused a shift in your thinking. "Alert," says your conscious mind, "check for alignment."

When anything like that happens, it means you are operating well. Relax, and go with the flow. Know that you are not having concentration lapses that signal early signs of a brain disorder.

Below are a few illustrations of possible ways to work as you build your model.

Example One: Ethan

Ethan is thirty years old. He has an MBA degree and a law degree, has passed the bar exam, and is working for a prestigious law firm in a major city. He earns an excellent salary and is highly regarded, both within the firm and with his clients. His career trajectory is enviable. He is unmarried and is not in a committed relationship.

But Ethan feels miserable.

He's doing well in a job and a career that he hates. He is a litigation attorney. He is upset by the contentious nature of his interactions with other people. The stress is affecting his physical and emotional health. He wants out. He is not driven by money, yet he pursues it. He cannot talk to his parents about his feelings because his mother and father are both successful lawyers, and they pushed him to follow in their footsteps, paid for his schooling, and helped him land his job. They would be disappointed and angry if he told them how he truly feels.

Ethan is lost. He desperately wants to change his life. He understands the What's Next model. It all sounds good on paper. But he doesn't know where to begin.

In reflecting on his life, Ethan has come to realize that he does not know who he is or what he wants out of life. His parents have chosen every pursuit and path in his life. His values are those of his parents. He feels as if he is a robot.

Ethan determines that he must begin his journey out of his current state by understanding who he is, what he believes in, and how he wants to define himself.

He will first determine and define his values. As Ethan proceeds to reflect on the values instilled in him by his parents, he discovers that some of his parents' values conflict with his own beliefs. He is surprised. Once he internalizes this discovery and is able to embrace this new truth, he feels angry at himself. How could he let this happen? Why, he asks himself, was he so numbed to his own feelings? More reflection reveals more truths.

As Ethan continues to discover his authentic self, his fog of uncertainty begins to clear. He can feel his power to control his destiny slowly emerging. Ethan begins to ask some "What would it take" questions: "What would it take for me to have the courage and confidence to break free of my drive for material success and find my own path to a fulfilling life? What would it take for me to have a painful but honest and necessary discussion with my parents without destroying our relationship?"

Ethan, becoming comfortable with a set of values that truly embody his beliefs, decides to focus on his greater purpose. He knows that finding his purpose will supply the confidence he needs to escape his unsatisfying life. He does not want to think about a vision until he feels more certain of his greater purpose.

And so goes Ethan's process, one step at a time, in the order that feels right for finding his balance, charting his course, and making the choices that will lead him to the fulfilling life he dreams of living.

Example Two: Joan

Joan should feel ecstatic about the opportunities in front of her. She just turned fifty-five, sold her boutique clothing company at a price that assures her financial stability for life, and has no obligations holding her back. She has been divorced for several years and has two adult daughters, each of whom are happily living their lives in different parts of the country.

But Joan doesn't feel ecstatic. Instead, she feels uncertain, fearful, conflicted, and confused.

When Joan was running her business, her life had certainty. She knew how she would spend every waking hour of every day. She enjoyed her life. But her success came at a personal price. Joan had to take on more and more responsibilities for her store's operations. With each milestone of success, she experienced increased pressure. Those forces built up over the years until Joan realized it was time for her to sell her business.

Ever since the sale, she awakens every morning with complete freedom and feeling clueless about what to do with that freedom.

She knew about the What's Next model. But how and where should she begin to build it? Vision seemed too vague to Joan, and she already felt grounded in knowing and living her values.

Greater purpose. Yes. She would begin there. That, she felt, would help her become more grounded. She will find paths to explore and experiment with activities she has never done. She might travel, something she did little of when her business consumed her. Seeing new places might spark new interests or offer new opportunities to consider.

So Joan set out to find her greater purpose. As she began to imagine opportunities, she found herself rejecting almost every idea she envisioned. Her self-limiting beliefs about what was possible were strangling her imagination.

She asked herself, "What would it take to trust my imagination and not be constrained by my self-limiting beliefs about what I can and cannot do?"

Joan quickly discovered that in truth, some of her values were holding her back. She realized she needed to revisit her values, perhaps abandon some and establish some new ones.

She shifted her focus, and as she did, she uncovered her need to adopt two new values that would support her journey going forward.

She decided she must become more curious and more adaptable, two traits that during her working career never entered her consciousness.

She thought deeply about what it would take to trust her instincts within the framework of her two new values—curiosity and adaptability. She wrote about this in her journal, and she began to clearly define her new values and the role they would play in her next chapter.

Her fear began to dissipate, replaced by confident curiosity. As this happened, she decided to return to search for her greater purpose. As she progressed, she began to think about the context of her greater purpose as it related to her vision of where she wished to be in ten years' time.

So went Joan's journey. Her process was shaped by a continuous shift in emphasis between her vision, her values, and her greater purpose. Her progress with each element stimulated her need to shift from one to another to maintain clarity, balance, and focus and to keep moving forward.

Example Three: Grace

Grace is a seventy-year-old, happily retired, socially engaged widow. She is in good health, physically active, and energetic. Three years earlier, after her husband's death, Grace's life plans had changed. The two of them had planned to travel, play golf, visit their children and grandchildren, and happily coast through their remaining golden years. Now Grace is looking for her own path.

During her working career, Grace had been a language teacher. She is fluent in English, Spanish, French, and German. After her husband's passing, she lost interest in travel and golf, and she became a private tutor. She taught English to several Spanish-speaking people whom she met through friends. She enjoyed teaching. It kept her busy.

Grace knows who she is. She lives her values, is confident, grounded, and busy, and she feels she had a purpose. But where was she headed? Grace felt something in her life was missing. She didn't want to simply coast along until someone was reading her eulogy. She wanted a destination, a more well-defined future reality. A vision.

One day, a neighbor approached her with a novel idea. The business he owned had a lot of customers in Mexico. He and his executives frequently traveled to Mexico City, and he thought it would be a good idea for all of them to learn to speak Spanish. He asked Grace if she would become their teacher. She did, and she loved it.

A concept was born. Grace began to test the water to see if she could expand her teaching activities. Of course, other companies were selling language programs, and some were highly successful. But throughout her years of teaching, Grace had developed some creative methods that made learning especially fun. She began advertising her unique kind of Spanish class through social media. People responded. Some asked her to provide classes in other languages, especially Chinese. Through prior teaching relationships, Grace found and hired people who were fluent in English and Mandarin, the most widely spoken Chinese dialect.

Grace now had a purpose and a vision. Given her health and vitality, she decided she never wanted to retire. Her vision was to create a unique boutique academy for English speakers who wanted to become multilingual citizens of the world. She knew she would find fulfillment in the process of creating and leading such an academy.

"What would it take" questions soon followed:

"What would it take to find capable people who share my vision who could help me build and lead this new entity?"

"What would it take to define the operating structure of my entity that would support its growth?"

"What would it take to maintain confidence and commitment through the challenges of early development?"

And Grace was launched.

A common thread runs through the three previous illustrations. All three people were guided by their inner voices. That is perhaps the most vital message: always listen to your inner voice.

Your voice will tell you in what order to proceed as you utilize the What's Next model. Your voice will tell you when to shift your focus and how to align the three elements—vision, values, and greater purpose. Your feelings and the emotions that shape them are not designed to be compartmentalized and controlled by a one-size-fits-all instruction manual. Rather, your inner voice will be your guide.

But be aware. You must always remember to consciously guard against the influence of your shadow values. They will continuously try to convince you to remain cozy and comfortable, to do nothing to change your status quo.

And every time, you must override them. Let curiosity overpower comfort. None of us learn or change or grow when our minds are not searching.

Let adaptability overpower your fear of being terrible as you begin to learn a new skill. The magic of neuroplasticity requires a lot of repetitive practice. Know that with diligence, you will progress from pathetic to okay to good and eventually to great. And in the process, you will grow.

Let your spirit of adventure overcome your self-limiting beliefs. Know that if you can dream it, you can do it.

In relation to everything in this book, and everything in life, you are a work in progress. No one ever completes the course of mastering life. Still, as you journey, make these choices.

Choose exciting over comfortable.

Choose passion over survival.

Choose being valuable over becoming irrelevant.

Now get out there and *be* the best version of your authentic self, *do* the things that take you where you have dreamed of going, and *become* one with your vision, your values, and your greater purpose.

Through it all you will discover that the joy of fulfillment is the truest measure of wealth.

And may your next chapter be your best chapter.

NOTES

Chapter 2

1. Research on neuroplasticity has shown that the brain has the remarkable ability to reorganize itself by forming new neural connections throughout life. This capacity allows for the rewiring of certain brain areas, which can be influenced by behavior, environment, emotions, and thoughts. Here are some key studies and findings that support the concept of neuroplasticity.

   M. M. Merzenich et. al, "Somatosensory Cortical Map Changes Following Digit Amputation in Adult Monkeys," *Journal of Comparative Neurology* 224, no. 4 (April 1984): 591–605. This foundational research by Michael Merzenich and his colleagues demonstrated that the sensory cortex in monkeys could reorganize itself in response to changes in sensory input. When a digit was amputated, the cortical area that previously responded to that digit began to respond to adjacent digits. This study showed that even adult brains could reorganize themselves, challenging the belief that brain plasticity occurred only during childhood.

   Bogdan Draganski et al., "Neuroplasticity: Changes in Grey Matter Induced by Training," *Nature* 427 (2004): 311–312. This study involved participants learning to juggle over three months. MRI scans before and after the training period showed increased gray matter in areas of the brain associated with visual and motor activity. This study demonstrated that learning new skills could lead to measurable changes in brain structure, even in adults.

   Richard J. Davidson et al., "Alterations in Brain and Immune Function Produced by Mindfulness Meditation," *Psychosomatic Medicine* 65, no. 4 (2003): 564–570. This study examined the brains of Tibetan monks who practiced meditation extensively. Using fMRI, researchers found that long-term meditation led to changes in brain activity in regions associated with attention and emotion regulation. This study suggested that mental training (like meditation) could induce neuroplastic changes in the brain.

Sara Lazar et al., "Meditation Experience Is Associated with Increased Cortical Thickness," *Neuroreport* 16, no. 17 (2005): 1893–1897. Researchers conducted MRI scans on people who meditated regularly and found increased cortical thickness in areas of the brain associated with attention and sensory processing. This study provided evidence that meditation could lead to structural brain changes, supporting the idea that mental practices can induce neuroplasticity.

Bryan Kolb and Robbin Gibb, "Brain Plasticity and Behaviour in the Developing Brain," *Journal of the Canadian Academy of Child and Adolescent Psychiatry* 20, no. 4 (2011): 265–276. This review highlights how experience and training can lead to structural changes in the brain's synaptic connections. It also discusses how these changes are linked to behavioral modifications and the recovery of functions after brain injuries. This study reinforced the idea that neuroplasticity is not only possible but can be actively harnessed for rehabilitation and skill development.

Norman Doidge, *The Brain That Changes Itself* (New York: Penguin, 2007). Doidge compiled multiple case studies showing how neuroplasticity can help people recover from strokes, learn new skills, and overcome brain damage. This book popularized the concept of neuroplasticity and brought attention to its potential for brain rehabilitation and personal growth.

Jill L. Kays, Robin A. Hurley, and Katherine H. Taber, "The Dynamic Brain: Neuroplasticity and Mental Health," *Journal of Neuropsychiatry and Clinical Neurosciences* 24, no. 2 (2012): 118–124. This research reviewed the impact of cognitive training and physical exercise on neuroplasticity in aging brains. The findings indicated that both activities could lead to cognitive improvements and structural brain changes. This study provided evidence that neuroplasticity continues into old age and that targeted activities can support brain health.

These studies collectively support the concept that neuroplasticity enables the brain to rewire itself in response to various forms of learning, experience, and practice. This has implications for everything from skill acquisition to recovery from neurological damage.

Chapter 6

1. Research on neuroplasticity has shown that the brain retains the ability to change and reorganize itself throughout life, supporting the idea that it can be rewired at any age. Here are some key studies and references.

   M. M. Merzenich et al., "Temporal Processing Deficits of Language-Learning Impaired Children Ameliorated by Training," *Science* 271, no. 5245 (1996), 77–81. Dr. Michael Merzenich's pioneering work in the field of neuroplasticity demonstrated that the adult brain can reorganize itself in response to new experiences, learning, or injury. His studies with auditory processing in monkeys provided foundational evidence for the brain's lifelong capacity for change.

   A. Pascual-Leone et al., "The Plastic Human Brain Cortex," *Annual Review of Neuroscience* 28 (2005): 377–401. This study showed how practicing tasks like playing the piano induces changes in the brain's motor cortex in adults, further validating that neuroplastic changes can occur in adulthood through practice and learning.

   M. Lövdén et al., "Experience-Dependent Plasticity of White-Matter Microstructure Extends into Old Age," *Neuropsychologia* 48, no. 13 (2010): 3878–3883. This research explored how environmental demands and interventions (e.g., cognitive training or physical exercise) lead to structural brain changes in older adults, suggesting that neuroplasticity persists even into late adulthood.

   R. J. Davidson and B. S. McEwen, "Social Influences on Neuroplasticity: Stress and Interventions to Promote Well-Being," *Nature Neuroscience* 15, no. 5 (2012): 689–695. These researchers demonstrated that neuroplasticity is involved in the brain's ability to adapt to stress and that mindfulness and meditation can enhance neuroplastic changes, even in older adults.

   Sara Lazar et al., "Meditation Experience Is Associated with Increased Cortical Thickness," *Neuroreport* 16, no. 17 (2005): 1893–1897. Research by Sara Lazar and colleagues found that meditation could lead to neuroplastic changes in the brain's gray matter, showing that mental training can alter the brain at any age.

   These studies affirm that neuroplasticity remains a lifelong process, and the brain can indeed be rewired at any stage of life.

ACKNOWLEDGMENTS

First and foremost I want to thank my wife, Arlene. She is beautiful, supportive, insightful, my best friend, soul mate, guardian of my healthy habits, and the force and inspiration behind having me write this book. Without her none of this would have come to be.

Many thanks and my deep appreciation to those who made this book possible.

My daughter Janet, for her insights and editorial guidance.

Amy Friedman, my editor whose skills made this book more readable and relatable.

Sharon Goldinger and her team at PeopleSpeak, for her expert guidance, strategy, and advice in making this book come alive.

Dr. Amir Vokshoor, for his support and for writing a compelling and heartfelt preface.

Jeff Turner, my friend and colleague, for his skills and contribution to the cover design and for helping identify a group of people for whom this book will be valuable.

Dr. Elizabeth Lindsey, for her support, her testimonial, and being a source of motivation and focus.

Stan Stahl, for his content contributions, support, and generous testimonial.

Tom Drucker, for his constructive input and photography skills.

Peter McDermott, for his patient help with the audio presentations.

And to the thousands of people I've met on my journey and with whom I've interacted. They helped me learn and grow and create the basis for this book, which I hope will help and inspire others on their own journeys to fulfillment.

INDEX

ABOUT THE AUTHOR

Bill Leider is a seasoned, highly respected executive leader, adviser, and consultant. He is the cofounder and managing partner of Axíes Group, a consulting company. He works with growth-minded leaders and organizations that want to propel their performance from acceptable to exceptional.

His more than forty years of experience include being the CEO of both publicly traded and privately owned companies, advising and consulting companies ranging from ambitious start-ups to Fortune 500s in a wide variety of industries, and coaching numerous executives to help them become more-effective leaders.

For the last ten years, Bill has been studying and applying the findings of neuroscience as they affect human interactions, the choices we make, relationships, and awareness of how our unconscious minds form our biases, direct our behavior, and instill in us our self-limiting beliefs. His work, combined with his business experience, has enabled him to develop a model to guide people through periods of profound, angst-ridden life changes that occur at various stages of our lives.

One day, Bill's wife, Arlene, suggested (hammered him over the head until he got the message) that his next book should address individual people and their journeys through the next chapters of their lives.

What's Next? was born.

Bill's previous two books, *Mastering Your Balance: A Guide to Leading and Living at Your Full Potential*, coauthored with Jason Thompson, his business partner, and *Brand Delusions: Exploding the Myths and Helping You Improve Your Brand—Professionally and Personally*, were critically well-received business books.

Bill serves on the advisory board of the Institute of Neuro Innovation, a neuroscience research organization involved in improving brain health in the area of depression. Bill also serves on the advisory board of SecureTheVillage, a nonprofit organization whose mission is to make the greater Los Angeles area the safest cybersecurity community in the United States.

He has lectured at the Sol Price School of Public Policy at the University of Southern California, where he taught leadership in counterterrorism as a required part of the Public Policy master's degree program.

On a personal note, Bill and Arlene pursue their interests in discovering new foods that are rich in healthy ingredients and don't contain refined sugar, gluten, or dairy—and they are delicious. Arlene has an amazing talent for creating the dishes, and Bill is her avid taste-testing pilot. They are also involved in meditation and diaphragmatic breathing. Their two dogs—Benny, a seventy-pound standard poodle, and Cha Cha, an eight-pound Italian Bolognese—make for an entertaining odd couple.